Workshop Linguistic Complexity and Natural Language Processing (LC&NLP-2018)

Santa Fe, New Mexico, USA
25 August 2018

ISBN: 978-1-5108-6918-9

COLING 2018

The 27th International Conference on Computational Linguistics

Proceedings of the Workshop on Linguistic Complexity and Natural Language Processing (LC&NLP-2018)

August 25, 2018
Santa Fe, New Mexico, USA

Copyright of each paper stays with the respective authors (or their employers).

Preface

The workshop on "Linguistic Complexity and Natural Language Processing" focuses on linguistic complexity and its relevance in the field of natural language processing. It is a cross-discipline workshop that foster exchange of ideas between people in the area of artificial intelligence and natural language processing and people dealing with natural language complexity from a cognitive or a theoretical point of view. The main objective of this workshop is to bring together researchers from different areas that have in common their interest on linguistic complexity (from a practical or theoretical perspective) boosting the interchange of knowledge and methods between specialists that have approached complexity from different viewpoints. We want to promote interdisciplinarity among researchers that are dealing with any type of language complexity.

Complexity has become an important concept in several scientific disciplines. There has been a lot of research on complexity and complex systems in the natural sciences, economics, social sciences and, now, also increasingly in linguistics. Moreover, linguistic complexity may be a key point in automatic natural language processing, since results in that field may condition the design of language technologies.

Are all languages equally complex? Does it make sense to compare the complexity of languages? Can languages differ in complexity? Complexity is a controversial concept in linguistics. Until recently, natural language complexity has not been widely researched and still not clear how complexity has to be defined and measured. Twentieth century most theoretical linguists have defended the equi-complexity dogma, which states that the total complexity of a natural language is fixed because sub-complexities in linguistic sub-systems trade off. This idea of equi-complexity, seen for decades as an unquestioned truism of linguistics, has begun to be explicitly questioned in recent years. There have been attempts to apply the concept of complexity used in other disciplines in order to find useful tools to calculate linguistic complexity. Information theory, computational models or the theory of complex systems are examples of areas that provide measures to quantitatively evaluate linguistic complexity.

Many models have been proposed to confirm or refute the hypothesis of linguistic equi-complexity. The tools, criteria and measures to quantify the level of complexity of languages vary and depend on the specific research interests and on the definition of complexity adopted. In fact, there is no agreement in the literature about how to define complexity. Instead, in the literature, we can find a variety of approaches that has led to linguistic complexity taxonomy: absolute complexity vs. relative complexity; global complexity vs. local complexity; system complexity vs. structural complexity, etc. Currently, there is no clear solution to quantify the complexity of languages and each of the proposed models has advantages and disadvantages.

The contributions to the workshop introduce new methods, models, definitions and measures to assess natural languages complexity (in human and automatic processing). They propose computational and formal approaches to linguistic complexity.

We would like to thank everyone who submitted a paper to the workshop, all the authors for their contributions, the members of the programme committee for their help in reviewing papers and, of course, all the people who attended this workshop.

We acknowledge the support given by the Ministerio de Economía y Competitividad and the Fondo Europeo de Desarrollo Regional under the project number FFI2015-69978-P (MINECO/FEDER, UE) of the Programa Estatal de Fomento de la Investigación Científica y Técnica de Excelencia, Subprograma Estatal de Generació de Conocimiento.

Leonor Becerra-Bonache, M. Dolores Jiménez-López, Carlos Martín-Vide, Adrià Torrens-Urrutia

Table of Contents

Workshop Program

Saturday, August 25, 2018

9:30–9:45   *Opening Remarks*

9:45–10:30   **Session 1**

9:45–10:30   *A Gold Standard to Measure Relative Linguistic Complexity with a Grounded Language Learning Model*
Leonor Becerra-Bonache, Henning Christiansen and M. Dolores Jiménez-López

10:30–11:00   *Coffee break*

11:00–12:30   **Session 2**

11:00–11:45   *Computational Complexity of Natural Languages: A Reasoned Overview*
António Branco

11:45–12:30   *Modeling Violations of Selectional Restrictions with Distributional Semantics*
Emmanuele Chersoni, Adrià Torrens Urrutia, Philippe Blache and Alessandro Lenci

12:30–14:00   *Lunch*

14:00–15:30   Session 3

14:00–14:45   *Comparing morphological complexity of Spanish, Otomi and Nahuatl*
Ximena Gutierrez-Vasques and Victor Mijangos

14:45–15:30   *Uniform Information Density Effects on Syntactic Choice in Hindi*
Ayush Jain, Vishal Singh, Sidharth Ranjan, Rajakrishnan Rajkumar and Sumeet
Agarwal

15:30–16:00   *Coffee break*

16:00–17:30   Session 4

16:00–16:45   *Investigating the importance of linguistic complexity features across different
datasets related to language learning*
Ildikó Pilán and Elena Volodina

16:45–17:30   *An Approach to Measuring Complexity with a Fuzzy Grammar & Degrees of
Grammaticality*
Adrià Torrens Urrutia

A Gold Standard to Measure Relative Linguistic Complexity with a Grounded Language Learning Model

Leonor Becerra-Bonache
Univ. Lyon, UJM-St-Etienne
Saint-Étienne, France
`leonor.becerra@univ-st-etienne.fr`

Henning Christiansen
Roskilde University
Roskilde, Denmark
`henning@ruc.dk`

M. Dolores Jiménez-López
Universitat Rovira i Virgili
Tarragona, Spain
`mariadolores.jimenez@urv.cat`

Abstract

This paper focuses on linguistic complexity from a relative perspective. It presents a grounded language learning system that can be used to study linguistic complexity from a developmental point of view and introduces a tool for generating a gold standard in order to evaluate the performance of the learning system. In general, researchers agree that it is more feasible to approach complexity from an objective or theory-oriented viewpoint than from a subjective or user-related point of view. Studies that have adopted a relative complexity approach have showed some preferences for L2 learners. In this paper, we try to show that computational models of the process of language acquisition may be an important tool to consider children and the process of first language acquisition as suitable candidates for evaluating the complexity of languages.

1 Introduction

In this paper, we propose to use a grounded language learning model for measuring the relative complexity of natural languages.

Complexity is a controversial concept in linguistics. Eventhough, natural language complexity has been extensively studied for almost two decades –starting with McWhorter (2001) paper published in *Linguistic Typology*–, it still not clear how complexity has to be defined and measured. The equicomplexity dogma, which stated that the total complexity of a natural language is fixed because subcomplexities in linguistic sub-systems trade off, has been almost completely debunked. We have seen what Joseph and Newmeyer (2012) name the "decline in popularity of the equal complexity principle". This situation has led to the proposal of many models, tools and criteria to quantify the level of complexity of languages (Dahl, 2004; Kusters, 2003; Miestamo et al., 2008; Sampson et al., 2009; Newmeyer and Preston, 2014). However, currently, there is no clear solution to measure linguistic complexity and each of the proposed models has advantages and disadvantages.

Criteria and measures of complexity remain unsolved and this may be due to the fact that there is no agreement about how to define complexity. Instead, in the literature, we can find a variety of approaches that has led to a linguistic complexity taxonomy: absolute complexity vs. relative complexity; global complexity vs. local complexity; system complexity vs. structural complexity, etc. With this diversity of definitions, measures and criteria to calculate complexity vary and depend on the specific research interests and on the definition of complexity adopted.

Proceedings of the Workshop on Linguistic Complexity and Natural Language Processing, pages 1–9
Santa Fe, New Mexico, USA, August 25, 2018.

In this paper, we adopt a relative approach to complexity. Specifically, from the following three different meanings of complexity that Pallotti (2015) identifies in the linguistic literature, we focus on the third one:

1. *Structural complexity*, a formal property of texts and linguistic systems having to do with the number of their elements and their relational patterns.

2. *Cognitive complexity*, having to do with the processing costs associated with linguistic structures.

3. *Developmental complexity*, the order in which linguistic structures emerge and are mastered in second (and, possibly, first) language acquisition.

From the two possibilities offered by the developmental meaning of complexity, we work on the second one, this is, we intend to calculate linguistic complexity by considering a child learner in the process of first language acquisition.

In order to calculate the relative complexity of language by taking into account the process of acquiring a language, we propose to use a computational model for first language acquisition. Specifically, we have chosen a machine learning model, since this kind of models deal with idealized learning procedures for acquiring grammars on the basis of exposure to evidence about languages (D'Ulizia et al., 2011).

In section 2, we introduce a language learning system to calculate linguistic complexity. The adequacy of this model for measuring linguistic complexity from a developmental point of view is based on the fact that the computational models developed in the area of grounded language learning can be useful for studying first language acquisition. An important advantage of grounded language learning tools is that they allow us to reproduce the learning context of first language acquisition. In fact, in these models we provide data to a learner, and a learner (or learning algorithm) must identify the underlying language from this data. This process have some similarities with the process of language acquisition where children receive linguistic data and from them they learn their mother tongue.

The model calculates the number of interactions that are necessary to achieve a good level of performance in a given language by using a unique algorithm to learn any language. Therefore, it allows us to calculate the *cost* –in terms of the number of interactions– to reach a good level of performance in a given language and offer the possibility to measure the *difficulty* of acquiring different natural languages, since it may show that not all the languages need the same number of linguistic interactions to reach the same level of performance.

Therefore, the grounded learning system introduced in section 2 may be a potential adequate tool to measure the linguistic complexity in *relative* terms. In fact, the unique algorithm used in the model to learn any natural language could be seen as somehow equivalent to the innate capacity that allows humans to acquire a language. Moreover, the learner –this is, the machine– has no previously knowledge about the language. The machine represents, therefore, the child that has to acquire a language by just being exposed to this language. To count the needed number of interactions for the machine to achieve a good level of performance in a specific domain of the language may be equivalent to calculate the child's cost/difficulty to acquire a language. Finally, to show that with the same algorithm not every language requires the same number of interactions may be interpreted (in terms of complexity) as an evidence to defend that the difficulty/cost to acquire different languages is not the same and, therefore, languages differ in relative complexity.

One of the main problems in order to use this language learning model to calculate linguistic complexity is the evaluation of the performance of the system. Two measures will be used to evaluate the learning system: correctness and completeness. The *correctness* is the amount of the learner's sentences that are in the set of sentences that denote correctly one object. The *completeness* is the amount of sentences that denote correctly one object and appear in the set of learner sentences. The problem with the model we use is that it is not trivial to specify which is the set of correct denoting sentences, this is, there is not a gold standard to evaluate the model. In order to solve this problem, in section 3 we present a language model that integrates grammar rules and contextual semantic (CS) knowledge in order to generate the gold standard that will be used to evaluate the performance of the language learning model introduced in section 2, allowing the utilization of that model to calculate the complexity of natural language.

The model described in this paper will be used to determine the level of complexity of a set of natural languages. This model will be able to provide quantifiable experimental results that may show that languages differ in their relative complexity.

2 A grounded language learning system to study linguistic complexity

Learning a language is a challenging task that children have to face during the first years of their life. The difficulty of this task is well described by the classic example given by Quine (1960). Imagine that a linguist visits a culture with a different language than his own, and a native speaker says "gavagai" while observing a scene with a rabbit scurrying by. To understand the meaning of this word, the linguist should figurate out if "gavagai" means "rabbit" or something else, such as the action performed by the rabbit or perhaps is just an expression used by the native speaker to catch his attention. Similarly, children learning their native language need to map the words they hear to their corresponding meaning in the scene they observe (Fazly et al., 2010). Hence, like in the previous example, children have to face, among others, the problem of *referential uncertainty* (i.e., they may perceive many aspects of the scene that are not related to the utterance they hear) and *alignment ambiguity* (i.e., to discover which word in the utterance refers to which part of the scene).

Taking into account all these aspects, Becerra-Bonache et al. (2015; 2016a; 2016b) developed an artificial system that, without any language-specific prior knowledge, is able to learn language models from pairs consisting of a *sentence* and the *context* in which this sentence has been produced. This type of learning is often called *grounded language learning*. This system is inspired by some research work developed by Angluin and Becerra-Bonache (2010; 2011; 2016). Note that these previous works were used in Jiménez-López and Becerra-Bonache (2016) to study the linguistic complexity of ten different natural languages, in *relative* terms (i.e., difficult/cost of learning a language).

In this section, we focus on the computational system developed by Becerra-Bonache et al. (2016a; 2016b), which uses a challenging dataset called *Abstract Scenes Dataset* (Zitnick and Parikh, 2013). It contains clip-art pictures of children playing outdoors and sentences that describe these images. This dataset was created using Amazon's Mechanical Turk (AMT). First, AMT workers were asked to create scenes from 80 pieces of clip art depicting a boy and a girl with different poses and facial expressions, and some other objects, such as toys, trees, animals, hats, etc. Then, a new set of workers were asked to describe the scenes using one or two sentences description; the descriptions should use basic words that would appear in a children's book. In total, the dataset contains 10.020 images and 60.396 sentences.

One of the main advantages of using abstract scenes versus real images is that they allow to study the scene description problem in isolation, without the noise introduced by computer vision tools while detecting objects in real images. Hence, the Abstract Scenes dataset allows Becerra-Bonache et al. (2016a; 2016b) to consider a scenario with a perfect vision system and focus on the language learning problem. In Figure 1, we can see an example of a scene, how the dataset encodes the objects in the scene and some of the human-written descriptions for that scene. It is worth noting that even if we know which objects are present in the image and their position, the alignment between clip-art images and sentences is not given, that is, we do not know which actions are depicted in the image (e.g., playing, eating) and which words can be used to describe them (e.g., s_3s.png is called *sun*)

The system developed by Becerra-Bonache et al. (2016a; 2016b) learns from (S, I) pairs, where S is a sentence that (partially) describes an image I. A sentence is represented as a sequence of words (n-grams). For the images, a basic pre-processing step transforms the information provided by the dataset (information given to the right in Figure 1) into a context C, by using a first-order logic based representation. Thus contexts are made up of a set of ground atoms that describe properties and relationships between the objects in the image. The meaning of an n-gram is whatever is in common among all the contexts in which it can be used. It is worth noting that a context describes what the learner can perceive in the world and, in contrast to other approaches, the meaning is not explicitly represented, the learner has to discover it. Hence, the input to the system is a dataset consisting on pairs (S, C) where S is a sentence

s_3s.png	0	3	469	31	2	0
p_7s.png	1	7	178	89	2	1
hb0_10s.png	2	10	100	250	1	0
hb1_4s.png	3	4	391	248	1	1
a_4s.png	4	4	205	98	1	0
c_7s.png	5	7	87	181	1	0
t_4s.png	7	4	279	115	1	1

"Mike is wearing a hat with horns", "Mike kicks a ball to Jenny", "An owl sits in the tree"

Figure 1: Example of an image extracted from the Abstract Scenes Dataset, its corresponding information (to the right), and three sentences related to the image (bottom).

related to a concrete C. Using inductive logic programming techniques, the system learns a mapping between n-grams and a semantic representation of their associated meaning. Experiments showed that the system was able to learn such a mapping and use it for a variety of purposes, including identifying the elements in a context that a sentence refers to and generating sentences describing a given context. For more details about the system and the experimental results, see Becerra-Bonache et al. (2016a; 2016b).

In this paper, we propose to use the artificial system developed in Becerra-Bonache et al. (2016a; 2016b) to study the complexity of languages from a relative point of view. This system is not only linguistically well motivated (for instance, the input given to the system has similar properties to those of the input received by children form their learning environment, and the system has no previous knowledge about the language to be learnt), but also allows to perform cross-linguistic analysis (a unique algorithm is used to learn any language, which could be equivalent to the innate capacity that allows humans to acquire a language). The question is: how to calculate the difficult/cost of learning a language by using this approach?

By following previous works (Jiménez-López and Becerra-Bonache, 2016), we could calculate the linguistic complexity in relative terms by counting the number of examples needed for the system to achieve a good level of performance in a given language. To evaluate the performance of the system, two measures can be used: correctness and completeness. Given a set of correct denoting sentences for a given image, the correctness of the learner is the fraction of learner's sentences that are in the correct denoting set, and the completeness of the learner is the fraction of the correct denoting sentences that appear in the set of learner's sentences. The problem with this approach is to define the set of correct denoting sentences for a given image, since it does not exist a *gold standard* to evaluate the system. In the next section section we present a solution to solve this problem.

3 A tool to evaluate the performance of the learning system

3.1 The language model

We use a language model that integrates grammar rules and contextual semantic (CS) knowledge. A *contextual semantic knowledge base (CSKB)* is a set of logical facts, giving a "flat" representation, cf. Hobbs (1985) and Christiansen and Dahl (2005b), which is well-suited for representing observable information about the objects, their properties and interrelationships in static scenes. Our model, that we call *Contextual Semantic Grammars* in the present paper, is symmetric with respect to deductive and abductive reasoning, implemented by standard logic programming technology. Grammar rules are given by the familiar Definite Clause Grammar notation (DCG, illustrated below) as they are available in Prolog, and the CSKBs may be represented and maintained by Constraint Handling Rules (CHR); see Christiansen and Dahl (2005a) for an introduction and Christiansen (2014) for a clarification of the theory behind this approach. We explain this by a small example; consider a Definite Clause Grammar consisting of the following, single rule, as part of a Prolog program.

```
greeting --> [roar], {present(bear)}.
```

The logical goal in the curly brackets is a condition that must hold for this rule to apply; thus analyzing the utterance `[roar]` with the `present/1` predicate given as a Prolog predicate will succeed when `present(bear)` is a fact in the Prolog program, and fail otherwise. Similarly, we can use the program to generate all possible `greetings`, which here would be either only `[roar]` or, if `present(bear)` is not true, the empty set. In this way, the program is used in a *deductive* way, with the semantic predicates interpreted *closed world*.

Declaring instead `present/1` as a CHR constraint predicates provides an open world interpretation, which overall leads an `abductive` analysis of given sentences. CHR is integrated with Prolog, executing in its normal top-down fashion, extended with a constraint store to which new constraints (such as `present(bear)`) are added when encountered by the Prolog interpreter; after execution, the resulting constraint store is printed out as answer; `phrase/2` is a Prolog built-in used to parse (or generate) a phrase according to the given DCG:

```
?- phrase(greeting,[roar]).
present(bear)
```

In other words, this answer can be taken as an abductive answer – the reason – why `phrase(greeting,[roar])` can be observed.

CHR includes also rules that govern the constraints in the store. While CHR originally was intended as a language for writing constraint solvers for numerical calculations and such – in which case it would be relevant to write CHR rules that define an equation solver – we use such rules to express general *semantic world knowledge*. In the CS Grammar used for our present experiments, each objects appearing in a scene has a unique identifier and a type, so, e.g., a bear will be represented by the two constraints, `object(ID)`, `type(ID,bear)`.[1] The following two rules indicate that the type of any object is unique and (by assumption about the clip-art images) that an image includes at most on bear. Logical variables are indicated by capital initial letters, thus distinguished from constants, predicates, etc.

```
type(ID,T1) \ type(ID,T2)  <=> T1=T2.
type(ID1,bear) \ type(ID2,bear)  <=> ID1=ID2.
```

Each rule applies as soon as constraints meeting the left side appear in the store; constraints following the backslash are removed, and those on the right side are added (in these examples, unifications are executed, perhaps leading to failure if a proposed interpretation is judged impossible). CHR has a variety of different rules and facilities, but the understanding of the details are not important for the present paper.

We can put these relationships into a logical formula as follows, considering a specific image.

$$Grammar \wedge WorldKnowledge \wedge CSKB \models \mathtt{sentence}(S)$$

For the present applications, *Grammar* and *WorldKnowledge* are fixed. Enhancing a given knowledge base by knowledge embedded in sentences means that *CSKB* is partially known, which we may write it as $CSKB_0 \wedge \mathit{?Extension}$, where the last component is unknown and filled in by an abductive interpretation of given sentences S.

Sentences may be approved or generated by a deductive analysis, i.e., *CSKB* is now the enhanced knowledge base effectively locked (close world) by converting it into Prolog facts. Here S is either a given sentence (for approval) or a logical variable that will be instantiated to alternative sentences by the execution.

Additionally, we may use the model to build part of the *WorldKnowledge* by analyzing a large collection of sentences for different images, for example to identify roles for verbs, e.g., which (types of) objects can eat and which are edible. However, we did not apply this for the present experiments.

3.2 Crafting a CS grammar for the clip-art image sentences

About 7000 images are given by partial descriptions, in the form of a CSKB for each image defining most of their objects and some – but not all – of their interrelationships. Each image is accompanied

---

[1]These identifiers may, as shown here, be new, unused variables, but when stored in a file to be loaded later, it is practical to replace such variables consistently by unique constant symbols.

by typically three sentences created by natural language users. We have – to some extent - manually corrected the corpus for spelling and grammatical errors and removed some sentences whose contents obviously went far beyond what is seen in the images.

As mentioned, our goal is, for each image, to extend the given CSKB with the knowledge embedded in the sentences about the image, such that we can generate additional sentences consistent with the image as well as checking whether sentences from other sources have this property.

A suitable grammar is developed in an iterative process combining general knowledge about the English language and the constructions and vocabulary used in the corpus. At each iteration the coverage (i.e., the percentage of all sentences that can be parsed) is checked and samples of the extended CSKBs are checked manually.

We can indicate the flavour of our Contextual Semantic Grammars, showing excerpts of our current version, involved in processing the sentence *"A red and yellow hot air balloon is floating over the park"*. Any constant symbols used internally to represent contextual semantics starts by the characters "c_"; for simplicity of writing the rules, we use generic predicates `rel` with one, two or three arguments for various relationships, say `rel(c_rain)` (*"It is raining"*), `rel(c_sleep, X)`, `rel(c_eat,X,Y)`.

First the grammar rules:

```
sentence --> subject(X,Number), vp(X,Number).
subject(X,Number) --> np(X,Number).
np(X,Number) --> det(Number,AnA), adjp(A,AnA), noun(X,Number,_), {rel(A,X)}.
det(singular,a)   --> [a].
det(singular,an)  --> [an].
det(singular,_)   --> [the].
noun(X,singular,a) --> [hot,air,balloon], {object(X), type(c_hot_air_balloon,X)}.
adjp(A1+A2,AnA) --> simpleAdjp(A1,AnA), [and], simpleAdjp(A2,_).
simpleAdjp(Ad, AnA) --> adj(Ad,AnA).
adj(c_red,a)      --> [red].
adj(c_yellow,a) --> [yellow].
adj(c_orange,an) --> [orange].
vp(X,Number) --> verb(V,intrans, Number), {rel(V,X)}, pp(X).
verb(V,Val,singular) --> [is], verb_ing_form(V,Val).
verb_ing_form(c_float, intrans) --> [floating].
pp(X) --> prep(P), np(Y,_), {rel(P,X,Y)}.
prep(c_over) --> [over].
noun(X,singular,a) --> [park], {object(X),type(c_park,X)}.
```

When the subject *"a ... hot air ballon"* has been recognized, the variable X in the first rule is instantiated to an identifier, which may be a new variable. This X is sent to the `predicate` and the pp subphrases, as they are expected to express further properties that are naturally associated with X.

The detailed analysis of the subject refers to the CS constraints `object(X)`, `type(c_hot_air_balloon,X)`. Operationally speaking, "refers to" here means that the constraints are created when in abductive mode, and checked when in deductive mode.

Notice that we allow only one or two adjectives in a row in a `adjp`, which fits with the given corpus and, when generating sentences, suppresses the creation of infinitely long sentences. The analysis of the `adjp` *"red and yellow"* additionally introduces, first `rel(c_yellow+c_red,X)` which in turn is reduced by a CHR rule shown below to `rel(c_yellow,X), rel(c_red,X)`.

The correct use of *"a"* and *"an"* is controlled by the arguments named AnA in the rules for np and `adjp`, see, e.g., the difference in the rules for adjectives `red` and `orange`. The rule for `adjp` indicates the principle that the choice of a/an follows immediately following word (adjective or noun).

The `predicate` gives rise to the CS constraints `rel(c_float,X)`[2] and the pp yields `object(Y), type(c_park,Y), rel(c_over,X,Y)`. A CHR rule introduces, as a consequences of the last one, also `rel(c_over,Y,X)`, which allows, in a next step, the generation of, say, *"The park is under the hot air ballon"*.

The Contextual Semantic Grammar includes also a collection of CHR rules, some that take care of operational needs such as avoiding loops and suppressing creation of duplicate constraints, and others

---

[2]It may be seen as a rather coarse simplification that we always attach proposition to the subject rather than the verb, but when using this grammar for analysis and generation we obtain results that look reasonable in most cases.

that express interesting knowledge. The processing of our chosen sample sentence involves activating the following rules.

```
rel(R,X) \ rel(R,X) <=> true.
rel(Rel1+Rel2,A) <=> rel(Rel1,A), rel(Rel2,A).
rel(c_over,X,Y) ==> rel(c_under,Y,X).
```

The first rule removes a duplicate constraint before any other rule is tried, which means that these rules also works together with the additional one `rel(c_under,X,Y) ==> rel(c_over,Y,X)` without looping.

4   Conclusions

In this paper, we have proposed to use a grounded language learning system –defined in Becerra-Bonache et al. (2015; 2016a; 2016b) for a different purpose– to study linguistic complexity from a developmental point of view. We have also introduced a tool for generating a gold standard in order to calculate the complexity of a language through the evaluation of the performance of the learning system.

Regarding the grounded language learning system, we may conclude that it presents several advantages to measuring linguistic complexity: it does not require any prior language-specific knowledge; it uses realistic data and psychologically plausible algorithms that include features like gradual learning, robustness to noise in the data, and learning incrementally.

In what refers to the tool for generating the gold standard, some final considerations are in order. As it appears, our grammar rules include several simplifications, but as is well-known, Definite Clause Grammars are quite flexible and there is a comprehensive literature since the 1970s on how to model various grammatical refinement. The additional use of CHR for abductive reasoning facilitates the use of a flat representation for the CS knowledge representation which avoids the difficulties of using a traditional compositional approach, involving that each sentence needs a meaning representation which is one huge structure covering the entire sentence; furthermore the entire contextual semantic knowledge base needs to be passed explicitly trough all phrases and subphrases.

In comparison to other approaches to abductive reasoning in logic programming, the present approach is note for its direct and efficient use of existing technology without any interpretational overhead. For a recent overview of Prolog based grammars, including the present ones, including lots of background references, see Christiansen and Dahl (2018).

The Contextual Semantic Grammars used in the present paper includes semantic information in a much simpler way, and the symmetry between abductive and deductive reasoning supports an intuition that every sentence reflects some underlying reality – as indicates by a particular clip-art image – independently of whether or nor this reality is known in all details to the language processor (whether human or machine).

As shown elsewhere (Christiansen et al., 2007a; Christiansen et al., 2007b), it is possible to integrate pronoun resolution in these sort of grammars, but in the present simplistic setting, there are very few pronouns that in most cases are resolved deterministically. For example, the only possible people are Mike and Jenny, so there is very little doubt to whom *"she"* refers.

In this paper, we claim that learning models can be seen as an alternative to the methods that have been used so far in the area of linguistic complexity. They are models that focused on the learning process and therefore open the door to consider children first language acquisition as the language use-type to calculate linguistic complexity. In general, recent work on language complexity takes an *absolute* perspective of the concept while the *relative* complexity approach –even though considered as conceptually coherent– has hardly begun to be developed. Computational models of language acquisition may be a way to revert this situation.

The proposed model may provide quantifiable experimental results and permits to perform crosslinguistic analysis. In order to determine the degree of complexity, we are working on experiments with a set of languages and we will be able to quantify the complexity of each language. Since our computational simulation allows us to reproduce exactly the same state/environment/requirements for the acquisition of any language we will assure crosslinguistic analysis regarding complexity.

Acknowledgements

This research has been supported by the Ministerio de Economía y Competitividad and the Fondo Europeo de Desarrollo Regional under the project number FFI2015-69978-P (MINECO/FEDER, UE) of the Programa Estatal de Fomento de la Investigación Científica y Técnica de Excelencia, Subprograma Estatal de Generación de Conocimiento.

The work of Leonor Becerra-Bonache has been performed during her teaching leave granted by the CNRS (French National Center for Scientific Research) in the Computer Science Department of Aix-Marseille University.

References

D. Angluin and L. Becerra-Bonache. 2010. A model of semantics and corrections in language learning. Technical report, Yale University.

D. Angluin and L. Becerra-Bonache. 2011. Effects of meaning-preserving corrections on language learning. In *Proceedings of the 15th International Conference on Computational Natural Language Learning, CoNLL 2011*, pages 97–105. Portland.

D. Angluin and L. Becerra-Bonache. 2016. A model of language learning with semantics and meaning preserving corrections. *Artificial Intelligence*, 242:23–51.

L. Becerra-Bonache, H. Blockeel, M. Galván, and F. Jacquenet. 2015. A first-order-logic based model for grounded language learning. In *Advances in Intelligent Data Analysis XIV - 14th International Symposium, IDA 2015*, pages 49–60.

L. Becerra-Bonache, H. Blockeel, M. Galván, and F. Jacquenet. 2016a. Learning language models from images with regll. In *Machine Learning and Knowledge Discovery in Databases - European Conference, ECML PKDD 2016*, pages 55–58.

L. Becerra-Bonache, H. Blockeel, M. Galván, and F. Jacquenet. 2016b. Relational grounded language learning. In *ECAI 2016 - 22nd European Conference on Artificial Intelligence, 29 August-2 September 2016, The Hague, The Netherlands - Including Prestigious Applications of Artificial Intelligence (PAIS 2016)*, pages 1764–1765.

H. Christiansen and V. Dahl. 2005a. HYPROLOG: A new logic programming language with assumptions and abduction. In Maurizio Gabbrielli and Gopal Gupta, editors, *Logic Programming, 21st International Conference, ICLP 2005, Sitges, Spain, October 2-5, 2005, Proceedings*, volume 3668 of *Lecture Notes in Computer Science*, pages 159–173. Springer.

H. Christiansen and V. Dahl. 2005b. Meaning in Context. In Anind Dey, Boicho Kokinov, David Leake, and Roy Turner, editors, *Proceedings of Fifth International and Interdisciplinary Conference on Modeling and Using Context (CONTEXT-05)*, volume 3554 of *Lecture Notes in Artificial Intelligence*, pages 97–111.

H. Christiansen and V. Dahl. 2018. Natural language processing with (tabled and constraint) logic programming. In Michael Kifer and Annie Liu, editors, *Festschrift for David S. Warren*. To appear.

H. Christiansen, Ch. Theil Have, and K. Tveitane. 2007a. From use cases to UML class diagrams using logic grammars and constraints. In *Recent Advances in Natural Language Processing (RANLP-2007)*, pages 128–132. Shoumen, Bulgaria: INCOMA Ltd.

H. Christiansen, Ch. Theil Have, and K. Tveitane. 2007b. Reasoning about use cases using logic grammars and constraints. In *Proceedings of the 4th International Workshop on Constraints and Language processing (CSLP 2007)*, number 113 in Computer Science Research Reports, pages 40–52. Roskilde University.

H. Christiansen. 2014. Constraint programming for context comprehension. In Patrick Brézillon and Avelino J. Gonzalez, editors, *Context in Computing – A Cross-Disciplinary Approach for Modeling the Real World*, pages 401–418. Springer.

O. Dahl. 2004. *The Growth and Maintenance of Linguistic Complexity*. John Benjamins, Amsterdam.

A. D'Ulizia, F. Ferri, and P. Grifoni. 2011. A survey of grammatical inference methods for natural language learning. *Artificial Intelligence Review*, 36(1):1–27.

A. Fazly, A. Alishahi, and S. Stevenson. 2010. A probabilistic computational model of cross-situational word learning. *Cognitive Science*, 34(6):1017–1064.

J.R. Hobbs. 1985. Ontological promiscuity. In William C. Mann, editor, *23rd Annual Meeting of the Association for Computational Linguistics, 8-12 July 1985, University of Chicago, Chicago, Illinois, USA, Proceedings.*, pages 61–69. ACL.

M.D. Jiménez-López and L. Becerra-Bonache. 2016. Could machine learning shed light on natural language complexity? In *Proceedings of the Workshop on Computational Linguistics for Linguistic Complexity*, pages 1–11.

J.E Joseph and F.J. Newmeyer. 2012. All languages are equally complex: The rise and fall of a consensus. *Historiographia Linguistica*, 39:2/3:341–368.

W. Kusters. 2003. *Linguistic Complexity: The Influence of Social Change on Verbal Inflection*. LOT, Utrecht.

J. McWhorter. 2001. The world's simplest grammars are creole grammars. *Linguistic Typology*, 6:125–166.

M. Miestamo, K. Sinnemäki, and F. Karlsson. 2008. *Language Complexity: Typology, Contact, Change*. John Benjamins, Amsterdam.

F.J. Newmeyer and L.B. Preston. 2014. *Measuring Grammatical Complexity*. Oxford University Press, Oxford.

G. Pallotti. 2015. A simple view of linguistic complexity. *Second Language Research*, 31:117–134.

W. V. O. Quine. 1960. *Word and object*. Cambridge, MA: MIT Press.

G. Sampson, D. Gil, and P. Trudgill. 2009. *Language Complexity as an Evolving Variable*. Oxford University Press, Oxford.

C.L. Zitnick and D. Parikh. 2013. Bringing semantics into focus using visual abstraction. In *Proceedings of the International Conference on Computer Vision and Pattern Recognition*, pages 3009–3016. Portland.

Computational Complexity of Natural Languages:
A Reasoned Overview

António Branco
University of Lisbon
NLX-Natural Language and Speech Group
Departamento de Informática, Faculdade de Ciências, Universidade de Lisboa
Campo Grande, 1749-016 Lisboa, Portugal
antonio.branco@di.fc.ul.pt

Abstract

There has been an upsurge of research interest in natural language complexity. As this interest will benefit from being informed by established contributions in this area, this paper presents a reasoned overview of central results concerning the computational complexity of natural language parsing. This overview also seeks to help to understand why, contrary to recent and widespread assumptions, it is by no means sufficient that an agent handles sequences of items under a pattern $a^n b^n$ or under a pattern $a^n b^m c^n d^m$ to ascertain ipso facto that this is the result of at least an underlying context-free grammar or an underlying context-sensitive grammar, respectively. In addition, it seeks to help to understand why it is also not sufficient that an agent handles sequences of items under a pattern $a^n b^n$ for it to be deemed as having a cognitive capacity of higher computational complexity.[1]

1 Introduction

The complexity of natural language became a specific topic of scientific inquiry and progress when it was addressed from the perspective of its computational processing. The study of the computational complexity of natural language was pioneered by Noam Chomsky in the late 1950's and has advanced since then with a growing body of established results.

This paper aims to provide a concise overview of these results. Its immediate motivation is the ongoing upsurge of research interest on the complexity of natural language. Examples of this interest include an edited volume on *Measuring Linguistic Complexity* (Newmeyer and Preston, 2014) and a special journal issue on *Pattern Perception and Computational Complexity* (Fitch et al., 2012b), and the reviews therein on *Computational Complexity in the Brain* (Chesi and Moro, 2014), on *The Neurobiology of Syntax* (Petersson and Hagoort, 2012) and on *Artificial Grammar Learning Meets Formal Language Theory* (Fitch et al., 2012a), among others.

In the context of this renewed interest many studies appear to be misled by misunderstandings of relevant mathematical notions and proofs, thus inducing misinterpretations of empirically gathered evidence. A case in point is the wide-spreading assumption that it is sufficient that an agent handles sequences of items under a pattern $a^n b^n$ or under a pattern $a^n b^m c^n d^m$ in order to ascertain ipso facto that this is the result of at least, respectively, an underlying context-free grammar or an underlying context-sensitive grammar. Another important related case to note is the assumption, more or less explicit, that an agent can be shown to master cognitive skills of higher computational complexity if it is shown to be able to handle a few sequences that conform to the pattern $a^n b^n$.

This paper aims at providing a reasoned overview on the computational complexity of natural language parsing. As these results are disperse within an array of publications, putting them together in an articulated presentation will allow these past advances to be beneficial to forthcoming research. In this regard, we also seek to reinforce the momentum around the topic of natural language complexity.

In the next Section 2, we report on how the intricacies of natural language processing have been circumscribed when it comes to address its computational complexity, and in Section 3, we present the criteria to ascertain different levels of computational complexity.

---

[1]This paper was partly supported by the PORTULAN/CLARIN Infrastructure and by the ANI/3279/2016 grant.

Proceedings of the Workshop on Linguistic Complexity and Natural Language Processing, pages 10–19
Santa Fe, New Mexico, USA, August 25, 2018.

The key evidence that supports the discussion around the level of computational complexity of natural language parsing is presented in Section 4, and how this evidence has received different interpretations and supported different research programs is discussed in Section 5. The paper closes with final remarks in Section 6.

The presented overview also has a dissemination purpose. In order to reach a broad audience, some formal details are left out. The references provided should allow interested readers to dive into the relevant details if they wish to explore them further.

2 Processing problems

Human language is an entity of the natural world and to know within which boundaries its computational complexity lies it is necessary to understand how its processing takes place, and vice-versa. There is various empirical evidence upon which to draw hypotheses about the processing of natural language. This ranges from latency times obtained in experimental settings from a population of subjects to individual linguistic judgments, and includes quantitative data collected from corpora or images and recordings of neurological activity in the brain, among others. In the current state of our scientific knowledge about natural language, the empirical data uncovered thus far have been accounted for by different hypotheses and research frameworks concerning the processing of natural language. To a certain extent, the cogency of the conclusions about natural language computational complexity are dependent on the corresponding framework-internal assumptions and primitives.

It is also worth noting that the processing of natural language is unlikely to constitute a single monolithic procedure. For instance, taking into account perception — which permits the mapping of a linguistic form into the linguistic meaning it conveys —, several procedures are likely to be involved and interacting among each other (e.g. the detection of the different phonemes, their grouping into individual lexemes, the grouping of lexemes into phrases, the compositional calculation of their meaning from the meaning of their parts, etc.) All such different dimensions and sub-problems of language processing do not have necessarily to be addressed by a single computational method or procedure, or by different solutions of the same level of computational complexity.

The chances of finding firm results on the complexity of language may thus be as much higher as the sub-procedure under consideration is simpler, and as the empirical evidence is more elementary and less controversial, i.e. less prone to possibly contingent framework-driven interpretation or accommodation.

Important results have been obtained when the issue of complexity is addressed by studying what is known as the recognition problem: given a string s of lexical forms of a natural language L, how complex is the procedure to determine whether or not s is a sentence of L?

Addressing the computational complexity of natural language from this perspective has the methodological advantage that the empirical evidence needed for its investigation is quite unequivocal and framework-independent, as it requires taking into account just strings of lexemes forming sentences.

One should not lose sight tough of this methodological option and of the possible scope of its contribution concerning the eventual understanding of the complexity of natural language. When put into perspective with respect to the vast intricacies of human language processing, recognizing a string of lexical forms as a sentence is certainly a simple sub-procedure. Other sub-procedures are expected to be called into play in the global processing of language. It is also worth noting that the overall level of complexity of human language processing is not lower than the level of complexity of its more complex sub-procedures, on the one hand, and on the other hand, it is possible that some of these procedures have higher complexity than the recognition procedure.

Thus, whatever results one may eventually arrive at when researching the complexity of the recognition problem, they should be taken as representing a lower bound of the overall computational complexity of natural language.

3 Complexity levels

For the sake of perspicuity, the recognition problem is rendered as a set membership problem. When for methodological purposes, the empirical evidence to be taken into account is confined to strings of lexemes, a language L lends itself to be regarded as the set S_L whose elements are precisely those strings of lexemes that are its sentences. Seeking a computational solution for the problem whether a string of lexemes s is recognized as being a sentence of language L is thus seeking a solution for the decision whether the string s is a member of the set S_L.

This would be a problem with an immediate, even if not efficient, brute force solution in case a human language could be extensionally presented as a listing with all and only its member sentences: it would simply require exhaustively scanning that list seeking for the input string. But as there is no clear size boundary for the possible longest grammatical sentences, that is not practically viable and the set of sentences of a language has rather been presented under an intensional definition. Such a definition relies upon a number of empirically motivated regularities and criteria determining the conditions for membership, which form a finite set of properly defined rules. This set of rules constitutes a grammar for the language.

Accordingly, a solution for the membership problem turns out to consist of designing a parser that takes as input a string s and a grammar G_L for the language L and after a finite number of steps delivers the answer *yes* in case s belongs to the set S_L defined by G_L, and the answer *no* otherwise. Under this methodological setup, a first move in assessing the computational complexity of the processing of a language consists of determining the complexity of the least possible complex parser for a grammar of that language.[2]

In this connection, it has been common practice to use a threefold computational complexity hierarchy as proposed by (Chomsky, 1956) that groups grammars into regular, context-free and context-sensitive types. All regular grammars are context-free grammars, and the set of all languages defined by the former are properly included in the set of all languages defined by the latter. Similar considerations hold with respect to context-free and context-sensitive languages, respectively.

In general terms that fit the purpose of the current overview, while no practical parser (i.e. with so called tractable computational complexity) could be found for every context-sensitive grammar, the best parsers for any regular or context-free grammar are practical solutions for the membership problem, with the best parser for regular grammars being a comparatively very efficient one.

In particular, the most efficient parsing algorithm for context-free grammars has polynomial (cubic) complexity, while best parsers for regular grammars have linear complexity — with time for obtaining a solution for a problem instance of size n (i.e. sentences with n lexemes) being around a value proportional to n^3 and n, respectively, in the worst case (Grune and Jacobs, 2007; Nederkhof and Satta, 2010; Pratt-Hartmann, 2010).

This complexity hierarchy has been a yardstick used to help determine the complexity of the solution for the recognition problem in natural language. Assessing the level of complexity for this solution turns out to thus consist of empirically clarifying what type of grammar is suited to cope with this problem.

4 Grammar types

The claim that natural languages are not strictly regular, i.e. that they are supra-regular, was put forward in (Chomsky, 1956), and empirical elements from the English language in support of it can also be found in (Gazdar and Pullum, 1987, p. 394), or in the more accessible textbook (Partee et al., 1993, p. 477). An argument can be presented as follows.

4.1 Supra-regular

Consider the following sequence of English example sentences built by successively embedding into each other direct object relative clauses modifying subjects:

The cat escaped.
The cat [the dog bit] escaped.
The cat [the dog [the elephant stepped over] bit] escaped.

---

[2]As possible starting points on this, see (Hopcroft et al., 2001; Sudkamp, 2006; Wintner, 2010). Some authors, like (Sampson and Barbaczy, 2014), stress the dynamic nature of grammars in individuals and that the set of sentences of a language may have flexible boundaries. Some parsing procedure is always in place though, that allows speakers to distinguish, for instance, between different dialects and variants of a given language.

The cat [the dog [the elephant [the mouse frightened] stepped over] bit] escaped.

...

Based on these examples, and letting

A = {*the dog , the elephant , the mouse , the fly ,...*}

B = {*bit , stepped over , frightened , chased ,...*}

be finite sets of simple noun phrases and transitive verbs, respectively, the following infinite sub-set of English can be defined

$$E' = \{the\ cat\ a^n b^n\ escaped \mid n \geq 0 \}$$

where a^n and b^n are any finite sequences of size n of concatenated members of A and B. Notice that E' is the intersection of the set E, containing all sentences of English, with the following regular language

$$R = \{the\ cat\ a^* b^*\ escaped\}$$

where a^* and b^* are finite sequences of any size of concatenated members of A and B, respectively. Given that regular sets are closed under the operation of intersection, that E' results from the intersection between R and E, and that E' is not regular,[3] hence set E, with English sentences, is not regular.

While it is not practically feasible to check this result for every one of the over 7 000 existing languages in the world (Lewis et al., 2015), it is worth noting that this argument has been easily replicated with other types of syntactic constructions besides the center-embedded relative clauses above, and also for natural languages other than English ((Gazdar and Pullum, 1987, p.395); (Partee et al., 1993, p.478)).

In this connection it is worth noting that (Fitch and Hauser, 2004), seconded by (Gentner et al., 2006), proposed that the divide between regular and supra-regular computational process is the key to tell the difference between non-human and human-like cognitive capacities. This claim was based on arguments of the sort just described.[4]

In the search for the possible place of natural languages in the Chomsky hierarchy of computational complexity, the above argument leads to the next compelling question, whether natural languages are not context-free, i.e. whether they are supra-context-free (besides being supra-regular).

4.2 Supra-context-free

For three more decades, different attempts were made to support the claim that natural languages are supra-context-free, resorting to data from English comparatives (Chomsky, 1963), Mohawk noun-stem incorporation (Postal, 1964), "respectively" constructions (Bar-Hillel and Shamir, 1964; Langendoen, 1977), Dutch embedded verb phrases (Huybregts, 1976; Huybregts, 1984; Bresnan et al., 1982), number Pi (Elster, 1978), English "such that" clauses (Higginbotham, 1984), or English sluicing clauses (Langendoen and Postal, 1985). Those that were to be eventually retained as the best arguments are based on reduplication in noun formation in Bambara (Culy, 1985), and on Swiss German embedded infinitival verb phrases (Shieber, 1985).[5]

The argument based on Swiss German data is as follows. Consider the following sequence of example sentences built by successively embedding verb phrases in subordinate clauses (-DAT and -ACC signal dative and accusative case, respectively):

---

[3] The proof that $a^n b^n$ is not regular resorts to the following Pumping Lemma for Regular Languages: Let L be a regular language. Then there exists a constant c (which depends on L) such that for every string w in L of length $l \geq c$, we can break w into three subsequences $w = xyz$, such that y is not an empty string, the length of xy is less than $c + 1$, and for all $k \geq 0$, the string $xy^k z$ is also in L (Hopcroft et al., 2001, p.126). Intuition for the proof: however the members of E' of length longer than c are broken, no subsequences of them can be found that consistently match a pattern $xy^k z$ (for a proof, see (Sipser, 2013, p.80)).

The intended proof that E' (and hence E, i.e. the English language) is not regular has its grip in case E' is considered to be infinite: see Section 5.2 below on the empirical grounds to eventually dispute this.

[4] The validity of the argument given the experimentally elicited data obtained to sustain it was strongly challenged however (Liberman, 2004; Coleman et al., 2004; Pinker and Jackendoff, 2005). An overview can be found in (Fitch et al., 2012a).

[5] For extended overviews and critical assessment, see (Pullum and Gazdar, 1982; Pullum, 1984; Partee et al., 1993).

Jan säit das mer em Hans es huus haend wele hälfe aastriiche.

Jan said that we the Hans-DAT the house-ACC have wanted help paint

Jan said that we have wanted to help Hans paint the house.

Jan säit das mer d'chind em Hans es huus haend wele laa hälfe aastriiche.

Jan said that we the children-ACC the Hans-DAT the house-ACC have wanted let help paint

Jan said that we have wanted to let the children help Hans paint the house.

...

Based on these examples, and letting

A = {*d'chind* , ...}
B = {*em Hans* , ...}
C = {*laa* , ...}
D = {*hälfe* , ...}

be finite sets of accusative noun phrases (A), dative noun phrases (B), accusative object taking transitive verbs (C), dative object taking transitive verbs (D), respectively, the following subset of Swiss German can be defined :

$$G' = \{Jan\ säit\ das\ mer\ a^n b^m\ es\ huus\ haend\ wele\ c^n d^m\ aastriiche \mid n, m \geq 0\}$$

Notice that G' is the intersection of the set G, with all sentences of Swiss German, with the following regular language R

$$R = \{Jan\ säit\ das\ mer\ a^* b^*\ es\ huus\ haend\ wele\ c^* d^*\ aastriiche\}$$

Given that context-free sets are closed under intersection with regular sets, that G' results from the intersection between R and G, and that G' is not context-free, hence the set G, with Swiss German sentences, is not context-free.[6]

5 Research programs

For the purpose of gaining insight into the computational complexity of natural language processing, the inquiry reported above focused on the complexity of recognizing a string of lexemes as a sentence. Its outcome turns out to be methodologically productive as it helps to uncover what appear as interesting constraints concerning the nature and processing of natural languages. The way these constraints have been addressed and accounted for has been a key factor on how different types of grammatical research frameworks for natural language have been shaped.

5.1 Matching the complexity of the recognition problem

One possible research path has been to study and design natural language grammars that match the claim of supra-context-freeness with as low a cost as possible in terms of computational complexity. This implies going slightly beyond context-freeness, just to the extent needed for the recognition problem of all sentences to receive a solution.

This goal has been pursued by exploring the fact that not all context-sensitive languages beyond context-freeness require a grammar whose parser is of non practical complexity.[7] Grammar formalisms of this type have then been used to develop computational grammars for natural languages able to handle known grammar constructions beyond the power of context-free grammars, thus providing a constructive

---

[6]The proof that $a^n b^m c^n d^m$ is not context-free resorts to the following Pumping Lemma for Context-free Languages: Let L be a context-free language. Then there exists a constant c (which depends on L) such that if z is any string in L such that its length is at least c, then we can write $z=uvwxy$, subject to the following conditions: (i) the length of vwx is at most c; (i) vx is not an empty string; (iii) for all $i > 0$, $uv^i wx^i y$ is in L (Hopcroft et al., 2001, p.275). Intuition for the proof: however the members of G' of length longer than c are broken, no subsequences of them can be found that consistently match the pattern $uv^i wx^i y$. (for a proof, see (Sipser, 2013, p.128)).

The intended proof that G' (and hence G) is not context-free has its full grip in case G' is considered to be an infinite set: see Section 5.2 below on the empirical grounds to eventually dispute this.

[7]For a critical overview, see (Gazdar and Pullum, 1987; Partee et al., 1993, Chap. 21).

argument that such linguistic constructions do not necessarily push the processing of natural language to computationally unpractical solutions.

This is the line of research pursued most notably i.a. by the GPSG[8] framework (Gazdar and Pullum, 1987), and by its successor, the HPSG[9] framework (Pollard and Sag, 1987; Pollard and Sag, 1994).

5.2 Approximating the complexity of the recognition problem

Another research path is based on a different position with respect to the interpretation of the results presented in the previous section.

First, it is worth noting that the more solid empirical evidence interpreted as possibly pushing natural language complexity beyond context-freeness is the so-called *cross-serial dependencies* mentioned above, with respect to Swiss German. It took not only almost three decades of research effort to arrive at the results reported in (Culy, 1985; Shieber, 1985), as no other kinds of constructions were identified as having the same sort of implication in terms of complexity. Moreover, the cross-serial dependencies between verb phrases and their complements get harder, if not impossible, to be recognized by native speakers beyond triple embedding (Shieber, 1985, p.329).

These circumstances have been invoked to support the view that natural languages are in their essence within the context-free level of complexity: put colloquially, a language that has a *finite* subset of sentences matching the pattern $a^n b^m c^n d^m$ (thus with $0 \leq n, m \leq k$ for some constant k), and that otherwise (i.e. expunged from that subset) can be described by a context-free grammar even when including that subset — note that *there is no requirement that the language be finite, only that the number of embeddings is finite*.[10]

Second, the *center-embedding constructions* pushing natural language complexity beyond regular grammar, in turn, are easy to replicate in different languages with different kinds of constructions. Nevertheless, also here, human speakers find themselves at odds to recognize sentences with more than a few embeddings. A vast arrays of empirical research results are confluent in reinforcing this observation, showing "that sentences with more than two centre embeddings are read with the same intonation as a list of random words, cannot easily be memorized, are difficult to paraphrase and comprehend, and are sometimes paradoxically judged ungrammatical" (Petersson and Hagoort, 2012, p.1976).

In this respect, it is interesting to note the contrast between, on the one had, the increasing difficulty of processing sentences in the sequence of center embeddings, used to argue for the supra-context-freeness of natural languages

> *The cat escaped.*
> *The cat [the dog bit] escaped.*
> *The cat [the dog [the elephant stepped over] bit] escaped.*
> *The cat [the dog [the elephant [the mouse frightened] stepped over] bit] escaped.*
>
> ...

and, on the other hand, the much lower difficulty in processing a syntactically similar sequence but now with *peripheral right-embedding*[11]

> *The cat escaped.*
> *The cat [that bit the dog] escaped.*
> *The cat [that bit the dog [that stepped over the elephant]] escaped.*
> *The cat [that bit the dog [that stepped over the elephant [that frightened the mouse]]] escaped.*
>
> ...

---

[8]Generalized Phrase Structure Grammar.

[9]Head-driven Phrase Structure Grammar.

[10]Intuition for the proof: (i) recall that by definition any grammar has *finite* sets of variables, terminals and rules, (ii) note that any string along a pattern of type a^n can be accounted for by n grammar rules of type $AN_i \rightarrow a \, AN_{i+1}$, with $1 \leq i \leq n$, and any sequence $a^n b^m c^n d^m$ can thus be accounted for with suitable successive application of the appropriate sets of rules of that kind, and (iii) recall that rules with the format $X \rightarrow a \, Y$ do not push grammars beyond the class of regular grammars (Sudkamp, 2006, p.196) and thus beyond the level of linear complexity in their application to the recognition problem.

[11]For an overview of literature reporting on this differing cognitive effort, as evidenced by longer processing times, experienced by human speakers in handling these two patterns, see (Chesi and Moro, 2014, Section 3). As an aside yet interesting note, for the same given level of nesting, center embedding is empirically found in (Bach et al., 1986) to be even harder to process than cross-serial dependencies of the type uncovered in (Shieber, 1985).

This contrast has been used to support the view that there might be a finite upper bound also for center embedding in natural languages, in which case a regular grammar should be enough to describe these linguistic constructions.

Mutatis mutandis, the observation above applies here: a language that has a *finite* subset of sentences matching the pattern $a^n b^n$ (thus with $0 \leq n \leq k$ for some constant k), and that otherwise (i.e. expunged from that subset) can be described by a regular grammar, can be described by a regular grammar even when including that subset. Again, note that *there is no requirement that the language be finite, only that the number of embeddings is.*[12]

This view is further reinforced by the fact that peripheral embedding, though not center-embedding, can be accounted for by regular grammars (Langendoen, 1975; Gazdar and Pullum, 1987; van Noord, 1998).

These points, together with the observation that humans process language very efficiently in a time that approximates a linear function of the length of the sentences, support the claim that regular grammars can provide at least very good approximations to the description of natural languages. This is the line of research advocated in (Roche and Schabes, 1997; van Noord, 1998).

Although they are different, it is worth noting that this perspective and the one indicated in the previous subsection are not necessarily in conflict. The complementarity nature of the two has actually been explored under the rationale that less complex solutions should be used as much as possible until the point where resorting to more complex solutions turns out to be unavoidable with respect to the eventual nature of the sub-problems to be solved. Regular methods have been applied to shallow linguistic processing, whose outcome feeds augmented context-free grammars in charge of deep linguistic processing, responsible for yielding fully-fledged grammatical representations (Crysmann et al., 2002).

Nevertheless, when it comes to the accommodation of the results presented in the previous section, the largest divide is perhaps not so much between these two research programs as it is between them and a third, to be presented in the next subsection below.

5.3 The complexity of the recognition problem in a trade off

The two approaches described in the two subsections above result from different perspectives on empirical data supporting arguments on the complexity level. A third line of research calls instead for putting into perspective the complexity metric used. In particular, it is noted that the distinction between polynomial and exponential is a coarse-grained measure of complexity, that is based on an asymptotic notation and abstracts away from many varying details of the basic operations of different computing devices. As repeatedly warned in textbooks on computational complexity, this distinction is known to be a reliable indicator of the actual superior efficiency of algorithms for problem instances that are larger than a sufficiently large size, such that a polynomial growth of the time needed to complete its operation will never be outperformed in terms of efficiency by an exponential growth.[13]

In the case of sentence recognition, the size of a problem instance is determined by the number of words in the input candidate sentence. And when it comes to natural languages, the actual input problem instances are made of at most a few dozen of words each on average.

Under such circumstances, for the actual time required to find a solution to a recognition problem instance of this size, it is likely that it is the natural language grammar — with its considerable memory size requirements in terms of the number of rules to be accessed, the internal data structure to encode them, etc. —, rather than the parser, that turns out to be responsible for the largest share. Moreover, moving from weaker and more efficient (e.g. regular) to more powerful and less efficient (e.g. context-sensitive) grammar types permits that a given language may be described more succinctly by its grammar. Consequently, grammars well beyond context-freeness — even if requiring companion, exponential parsers — may process natural language *sentences of actual average size* faster than infra-context-sensitive ones.

Thus, given the comparatively very small size of the actual input to the recognition problem in natural languages (the average size of sentences), the key issue for matching the observed human parsing effi-

---

[12]The intuition for the proof is as in footnote 10.

[13]As possible starting points on this, see among many others ((Guttag, 2013, Chap. 9) ; (Cormen et al., 2009, Chap. 3)) .

ciency is not finding the most efficient parsing algorithm to cope with the empirically observed data like those illustrated in the section above. Alternatively, it is finding the best trade-off between the level of complexity brought into the *overall sentence processing procedure* by the parsing algorithm, on the one hand, and on the other hand by other factors relevant given the small size of the input problems at stake — namely by the size and shape of the grammar. Accordingly, natural language grammar is very likely to be of a context-sensitive type, with its companion parser of exponential complexity.

This position is fully articulated in (Berwick and Weinberg, 1982).[14] The LFG[15] framework (Kaplan and Bresnan, 1982) is a research program that lends itself to be classified as a grammar framework admitting context-sensitive grammars for natural languages (Bresnan et al., 1982; Berwick, 1982).[16]

6 Final remarks

The programs of research on natural language grammar described above adopt different ways to accommodate results from research on the computational complexity of the recognition problem. Given the Chomsky complexity hierarchy for computable solutions, they fill the whole spectrum of hypothesis ranging from the position that the grammars of natural languages are regular to the positions that they are context-sensitive, also including the claim that they are basically context-free.

What these research programs and the argumentation supporting them bring to light is that, importantly, it is by no means sufficient that a linguistic construction instantiates, a language includes, or an agent handles sequences of items under a pattern $a^n b^n$ or under a pattern $a^n b^m c^n d^m$ to ascertain ipso facto that these patterns are the result or empirical evidence of at least, respectively, an underlying context-free grammar or an underlying context-sensitive grammar. Likewise, by themselves alone, they are not sufficient to ascertain cognitive skills of higher computational complexity.

To interpret the relevant empirical evidence here, *it is not only the shape of the patterns that matter; the possible length of the stretch made of iterated items and the size range of the input also matter.*

Of course, these observations also hold for artificial languages that happen to be mastered by humans and non-humans alike under experimental settings.[17]

Overlooking these results and research programs has misled many research efforts into a maze of misunderstandings of mathematical notions and proofs, and of concomitant misinterpretations of empirical data. This may very well be prolonged by the current revival of interest on the complexity of natural languages, with the programmatic insistence on pattern shape and with the continued overlooking of size and related efficiency issues (Fitch et al., 2012a; Chesi and Moro, 2014).

This should not, however, dispute that restricting the focus of inquiry to the recognition procedure has been a productive methodological move, one that has permitted new insights into the computational complexity of natural language. Yet, as noted at the outset, this is certainly just one of the possible subprocedures involved in the wider task of natural language processing, helping to advance research on the lower bound of natural language complexity.

As *empirical data from more and, above all, better articulated sources of evidence* become available (e.g. contrasts in grammatical judgments, linguistic performance and behavioral scores, records of brain activity, neurological findings, etc.), one should expect that the number of working hypotheses about the computational complexity of natural language could be narrowed down provided that they are obtained in experimentation correctly informed by the underpinnings of parsing methodology and of the theory of computation.

---

[14]Though inspired by other kind of empirical evidence, in the overview in (Petersson and Hagoort, 2012, p.1976), this is also what seems to be hinted at as an admissible hypothesis: "There are often interesting complex trade-offs between processing time and memory use in computational tasks, and understanding these might be of importance to neurobiology".

[15]Lexical Functional Grammar.

[16]The GB (Government and Binding) research framework and its successors in the scope of MP (Minimalist Program) (Chomsky, 1981; Chomsky, 1995) are deemed to embrace this position. These research traditions have been criticized though by not using a clearly defined grammar formalism, which could support the development of a computational grammar for which complexity issues can be determined (Johnson and Lappin, 1997; Johnson and Lappin, 1999; Lappin et al., 2000).

[17]For an overview on experimentation with artificial grammar learning, see ((Petersson and Hagoort, 2012);(Fitch et al., 2012a, Sections 5 and 6)).

References

Emmon Bach, Colin Brown, and William Marslen-Wilson. 1986. Crossed and nested dependencies in German and dutch: a psycholinguistic study. *Language and Cognitive Processes*, 1(4):249–262.

Yehoshua Bar-Hillel and E. Shamir. 1964. Finite state languages: Formal representations and adequacy problems. In Yehoshua Bar-Hillel, editor, *Language and Information*, pages 87–98. Addison-Wesley.

Robert Berwick and Amy Weinberg. 1982. Parsing efficiency, computational complexity, and the evaluation of grammatical theories. *Linguistic Inquiry*, 13:165–191.

Robert Berwick. 1982. Computational complexity and lexical functional grammar. *American Journal of Computational Linguistics*, 8:97–109.

J. Bresnan, R. Kaplan, S. Peters, and A. Zaenen. 1982. Cross-serial dependencies in dutch. *Linguistic Inquiry*, 13.

C. Chesi and A. Moro. 2014. Measuring linguistic complexity. In Newmeyer and Preston (eds.), Chap. 13.

Noam Chomsky. 1956. Three models for the description of language. *IRE Transactions on Information Theory*.

Noam Chomsky, 1963. *Formal Properties of Grammars*, pages 323–418. John Wiley And Sons, Inc. In R. Luce, R. Bush and E. Galanter (eds.), Handbook of Mathematical Psychology.

Noam Chomsky. 1981. *Lectures on Government and Binding*. Dordrecht, Foris.

Noam Chomsky. 1995. *The Minimalist Program*. MIT Press, Cambridge.

John Coleman, Greg Kochanski, Burton Rosner, and Esther Grabe. 2004. January. Letter to Science editor, http://kochanski.org/gpk/papers/2004/FitchHauser/FitchHauserScienceLetter.pdf Expanded in http://kochanski.org/gpk/papers/2004/FitchHauser/.

Thomas Cormen, Charles Leiserson, and Ronald Rivest. 2009. *Introduction to Algorithms*. MIT Press, 3rd edition.

B. Crysmann, A. Frank, K. Bernd, S. Mueller, G. Neumann, J. Piskorski, U. Schaefer, M. Siegel, H. Uszkoreit, F. Xu, M. Becker, and H. Krieger. 2002. An integrated archictecture for shallow and deep processing. In *40th Annual Meeting of the Association for Computational Linguistics*, pages 441–448. ACL.

Christopher Culy. 1985. The complexity of the vocabulary of bambara. *Linguistics and Philosophy*, 8:345–351.

Jon Elster. 1978. *Logic and Society: Contradictions and Possible Worlds*. New York.

W. Tecumseh Fitch and Marc Hauser. 2004. Computational constraints on syntactic processing in a nonhuman primate. *Science*, 303:377–380.

W. Tecumseh Fitch, Angela Friederici, and Peter Hagoort. 2012a. Artificial grammar learning meets formal language theory: an overview. *Philosophical Transactions of the Royal Society*, 367:1933–1955.

W. Tecumseh Fitch, Angela D. Friederici, and Peter Hagoort. 2012b. Pattern perception and computational complexity (special issue). *Philosophical Transactions of the Royal Society B*, 367.

Gerald Gazdar and Geoffrey Pullum. 1987. Computationally relevant properties of natural languages and their grammars. *New Generation Computing*, pages 387–43.

Timothy Gentner, Kimberly Fenn, Daniel Margoliash, and Howard C. Nusbaum. 2006. Recursive syntactic pattern learning by songbirds. *Nature*, 440:1204–1207.

Dick Grune and Ceriel Jacobs. 2007. *Parsing Techniques: A Practical Guide*. Springer.

John Guttag. 2013. *Introduction to Computation and Programming Using Python*. The MIT Press.

James Higginbotham. 1984. English is not a context-free language. *Linguistic Inquiry*, 15:225–234.

J. Hopcroft, R. Motwani, and J. Ullman. 2001. *Introduction to Automata Theory, Languages, and Computation*.

R. Huybregts. 1976. Overlapping dependencies in dutch. Number 1. pp.24-65.

Riny Huybregts. 1984. The weak inadequacy of context-free phrase structure grammars. In Germen J. de Haan, Mieke Trommelen, and Wim Zonneveld, editors, *Van Periferie Naar Kern*, pages 81–99. Foris Publications.

David Johnson and Shalom Lappin. 1997. A critique of the minimalist program. *Linguistics and Philosophy*, 20:273–333.

David Johnson and Shalom Lappin. 1999. *Local Constraints vs Economy*. CSLI Publications.

Ronald Kaplan and Joan Bresnan. 1982. Lexical-functional grammar: A formal system for grammatical representation. In Joan Bresnan, editor, *The Mental Representation of Grammatical Relations*, pages 173–281.

Terence Langendoen and Paul Postal. 1985. English and the class of context-free languages. *Computational Linguistics*, 10:177–181.

Terence Langendoen. 1975. Finite-state parsing of the phrase-structure languages and the status of readjustment rules in grammar. *Linguistic Inquiry*, 5:533–554.

Terence Langendoen. 1977. On the inadequacy of type-2 and type-3 grammars for huiman languages. In P. Hopper, editor, *Studies in Descriptive and Historical Linguistics*. John Benjamins.

Shalom Lappin, Robert Levine, and David Johnson. 2000. The structure of unscientific revolutions. *Natural Language and Linguistic Theory*, 18:665–771.

M. Paul Lewis, Gary F. Simons, and Charles D. Fennig, editors. 2015. *Ethnologue, Languages of the World*. SIL International, 18th edition.

Marc Liberman. 2004. *Humans context-free, monkeys finite-state? Apparently not*. Language Log.

Mark Nederkhof and Giorgio Satta. 2010. Theory of parsing. pages 105–130. In A. Clark, C. Fox and S. Lappin (eds.), The Handbook of Computational Linguistics and Natural Language Processing, Chap. 4.

Frederick J. Newmeyer and Laurel B. Preston, editors. 2014. *Measuring Linguistic Complexity*. OUP.

Barbara Partee, Alice ter Meulen, and Robert Wall. 1993. *Mathematical Methods in Linguistics*. Kluwer.

Karl Magnus Petersson and Peter Hagoort. 2012. The neurobiology of syntax: beyond string sets. *Philosophical Transactions of the Royal Society*, 367:1933–1955.

Steven Pinker and Ray Jackendoff. 2005. The faculty of language: What's special about it? *Cognition*, 95:201–36.

Carl Pollard and Ivan Sag. 1987. Information-based syntax and semantics. *CSLI Publication*.

Carl Pollard and Ivan Sag. 1994. *Head-Driven Phrase Structure Grammar*. The University of Chicago.

Paul Postal. 1964. Limitations of phrase structure. In J. Fodor and J. Katz, editors, *The Structure of Language: Readings in the Philosophy*. Englewood Cliffs, Prentice-Hall.

Ian Pratt-Hartmann. 2010. Computational complexity in natural language. pages 43–73. In A. Clark, C. Fox and S. Lappin (eds.), The Handbook of Computational Linguistics and Natural Language Processing, Chap. 2.

Geoffrey Pullum and Gerald Gazdar. 1982. Natural languages and context-free languages. *Linguistics and Philosophy*, 4:471–504.

Geoffrey Pullum. 1984. On two recent attempts to show that english is not a cfl. *Computational Linguistics*, 10:182–188.

Emmanuel Roche and Yves Schabes. 1997. *Finite-State Language Processing*. The MIT Press.

Geoffrey Sampson and Anna Barbaczy. 2014. *Grammar without Grammaticality: growth and limits of grammatical precision*. De Gruyter Mouton, Berlin.

Stuart Shieber. 1985. Evidence against the context-freeness of natural language. *Linguistics and Philosophy*, 8:333–343.

Michel Sipser. 2013. *Introduction to the Theory of Computation*. Cengage Learning, 3rd edition.

Thomas A. Sudkamp. 2006. *Languages and Machines: An Introduction to the Theory of Computer Science*. Pearson, Boston.

Gertjan van Noord. 1998. *Algorithms for Linguistic Processing*. Alfa-informatica, Groningen. http://odur.let.rug.nl/ vannoord/alp/proposal/pion.html.

Shuly Wintner. 2010. Formal language theory. pages 11–42. Wiley-Blackwell. In Alexander Clark, Chris Fox and Shalom Lappin (eds.), The Handbook of Computational Linguistics and Natural Language Processing, Chap. 4.

Modeling Violations of Selectional Restrictions
with Distributional Semantics

Emmanuele Chersoni
Aix-Marseille University
emmanuelechersoni@gmail.com

Adrià Torrens Urrutia
Universitat Rovira i Virgili
adria.torrens@urv.cat

Philippe Blache
Aix-Marseille University
philippe.blache@univ-amu.fr

Alessandro Lenci
University of Pisa
alessandro.lenci@unipi.it

Abstract

Distributional Semantic Models have been successfully used for modeling selectional preferences in a variety of scenarios, since distributional similarity naturally provides an estimate of
the degree to which an argument satisfies the requirement of a given predicate. However, we
argue that the performance of such models on rare verb-argument combinations has received relatively little attention: it is not clear whether they are able to distinguish the combinations that are
simply atypical, or implausible, from the *semantically anomalous* ones, and in particular, they
have never been tested on the task of modeling their *differences in processing complexity*.
In this paper, we compare two different models of thematic fit by testing their ability of identifying *violations of selectional restrictions* in two datasets from the experimental studies.

1 Introduction

In recent years, Distributional Semantic Models (henceforth DSMs) have been at the core of one of the
most active research areas in NLP, and have been applied to a wide variety of tasks. Among these, distributional modeling of selectional preferences (Erk et al., 2010; Baroni and Lenci, 2010) has been quite
popular in computational psycholinguistics, since the similarity estimated by DSMs works very well for
predicting the *thematic fit* between an argument and a verb. That is to say, the more the argument vector
is similar to some kind of vector representation of the ideal filler of the verb slot (it can be either an abstract prototype, or a cluster of exemplars), the more the argument will satisfy the semantic requirements
of the slot. The notion of thematic fit, as it has been proposed by the recent psycholinguistic research [1],
is related to, but not totally equivalent to the classical notion of selectional preferences, since the former
refers to a gradient compatibility between verb and role, whereas the latter conceives such compatibility
as as boolean constraint evaluated on discrete semantic features (Lebani and Lenci, 2018).

The distributional models of thematic fit have been evaluated by comparing the plausibility scores
produced by the models with human-elicited judgements (Erk et al., 2010; Baroni and Lenci, 2010;
Greenberg et al., 2015; Santus et al., 2017), showing significant correlations. Moreover, they have been
used to predict the composition and the update of argument expectations (Lenci, 2011; Chersoni et al.,
2016), and for modeling reading times of experimental studies on complement coercion (Zarcone et al.,
2013). However, an issue regarding their evaluation has not been addressed yet, i.e. their ability of
capturing *different levels of implausibility*. [2]

Our processing system is sensitive to minimal variations in predictability between highly unpredictable
word combinations, and such sensitivity has been shown to have an influence on reading times (Smith and
Levy, 2013). Moreover, word combinations that are simply rare and/or unlikely and word combinations
that are semantically deviant have been shown to have different consequences on processing complexity
(Paczynski and Kuperberg, 2012; Warren et al., 2015).

---

[1] See McRae and Matsuki (2009) for an overview.

[2] A partial exception is the study on semantic deviance by Vecchi et al. (2011). However, they focus on the acceptability of
adjectival phrases, rather than on selectional preferences.

20

Proceedings of the Workshop on Linguistic Complexity and Natural Language Processing, pages 20–29
Santa Fe, New Mexico, USA, August 25, 2018.

From this point of view, thematic fit models represent an interesting alternative to the traditional probabilistic ones: they use distributional information about typical arguments to create an abstract representation of the "ideal" filler of the argument slot, and thus they are more capable of generalizing to the unseen. In other words, it does not matter if a specific verb-argument combination is attested in the training corpus of our system or not: its plausibility will still be computed on the basis of the similarity of the argument with the words that typically satisfy the requirements of the verb. It is important to stress that the inability to work with rare expressions has been for a long time a general point of criticism of statistical approaches to language, precisely because they could not explain why a given linguistic expression is not attested in the data (Vecchi et al., 2011).

In the present contribution, we take the first step toward the evaluation of thematic fit models on semantic anomaly detection. We set up a simple classification task on two datasets that have been recently introduced in the literature, and we test two different models on their ability to discriminate between a typical anomalous condition, i.e. **the violation of a selectional restriction**, and other highly unpredictable conditions.

2 Related Work

2.1 Distributional Semantic Models

All the DSMs rely on some version of the *Distributional Hypothesis* (Lenci, 2008), which can be stated as follows: *The semantic similarity between two linguistic expressions A and B is a function of the similarity of the linguistic contexts in which A and B occur.*

The idea of analyzing meaning by measuring the similarity of distributional patterns turned out to be one of the most successful in the computational semantics research of the last two decades. Thanks to the improvements of automatic tools for language analysis and to the online availability of huge *corpora* of text, it has become easier and easier to automatically derive semantic representations of linguistic expressions in the form of *vectors* recording their contexts of occurrence. The closer two vectors in a distributional space, the more similar the meanings of the corresponding words.

Depending on the task, different definitions can be given to the notion of context: the contexts for a target word can be simply other words co-occurring within a sentence, within a word window with a fixed size or, as in our case, words that are syntactically related. In their most classical form, the so-called **Structured DSMs** use *syntactic relation: word* pairs as contexts to represent linguistic expressions. For example, *subject:baby, adverb: loudly* are possible contexts for the distributional representation of the verb *to cry*.

Since most DSMs of selectional preferences are structured and based on dependencies, also the models presented in this work will share the same features.

2.2 Thematic Fit and Distributional Semantics

Given a specific verb role-argument combination, the thematic fit task generally consists in predicting a value that expresses how well the argument fits the requirements of the role, e.g. how good is *burglar* as a patient for *arrest*. Since Erk et al. (2010), thematic fit models have been typically evaluated in terms of correlation of the model-derived scores with human-elicited judgements that have been collected for the purpose of psycholinguistic experiments (McRae et al., 1998; Ferretti et al., 2001; Padó, 2007; Hare et al., 2009). Erk and colleagues computed the fit of the candidate nouns by assessing their similarity with previously attested fillers of the respective roles. Going back to the previous example, if *burglar* is distributionally similar to the nouns of the entities that are typically *arrested*, then it should get a high score.

Baroni and Lenci (2010) similarly evaluated their Distributional Memory (DM) framework on the same task, adopting an approach that has became very popular in the literature: for each verb role, they built a single prototype vector by averaging the dependency-based vectors of its most typical fillers. The higher the similarity of a noun with a role prototype, the higher its plausibility as a filler for that role. Their model inspired several other studies: some of them tried to refine their DSM by using semantic roles-based vectors instead of dependency-based ones (Sayeed and Demberg, 2014; Sayeed et al., 2015) or by using multiple prototypes, obtained through hierarchical clustering of the role fillers, in order to deal with verb polysemy (Greenberg et al., 2015).

An extension of the original model, introduced by Lenci (2011), has also been used to compute the dynamic update on the expectations for an argument filler, depending on how other roles have been filled in the previous part of the sentence (i.e., *engine* and *spelling* are both good patients for *to check*, but if the agent slot is filled by *mechanic*, then the former becomes a more predictable patient than the latter), and tested his system in a binary classification task on the subject-verb-object triples of the Bicknell dataset (Bicknell et al., 2010). More recently, Chersoni et al. (2016) integrated a similar mechanism of thematic fit computation in a more general model of semantic complexity, and obtained results comparable to Lenci (2011) on the same dataset.

Finally, Zarcone et al. (2013) made use of the notion of thematic fit in their study on complement coercion. Typically, we have a *complement coercion* when an event-selecting verb takes an entity-denoting NP as its direct object (i.e. *the author began the book*), so that a hidden verb has to inferred in order to satisfy the selectional restrictions of the verb (*the author began **writing** the book*). These authors computed the thematic fit for different verb-object combinations, corresponding to the experimental items used in the psycholinguistic experiments of McElree et al. (2001) and Traxler et al. (2002), and showed that the scores mirrored very closely the differences across conditions that were found in the above-mentioned studies. The coercion condition is particularly interesting for the present work, since it consists of an apparent violation of selectional restrictions. Therefore, the discrimination between actual violations and cases of complement coercion will be one of the tests for our models.

2.3 Experimental Evidence on Selectional Restrictions

Selectional restrictions can be defined as the set of semantic features that a verb requires of its arguments (Warren et al., 2015). Modular theories argued that they were represented in the lexicon, which was seen as a specialized module (Katz and Fodor, 1963; Fodor, 1983): it was generally assumed that the human comprehension system initially uses the knowledge available in such modules, and only later uses general world knowledge.

Since now there is evidence speaking against the modularity of the lexicon (Nieuwland and Van Berkum, 2006) and in favor of the access to world knowledge in the early stages of the comprehension process (McRae et al., 1998; McRae and Matsuki, 2009), it was questioned whether selectional restrictions have an independent reality, instead of being just part of a general world knowledge about events and participants (Hagoort et al., 2004; Kuperberg, 2007).

However, an EEG experiment by Pacyznski and Kuperberg (2012) showed that the processing difficulty of a sentence is affected differently by violation of selectional restrictions, with respect to simple event knowledge violation. The authors recorded ERPs on post-verbal Agent arguments as participants read passive English sentences, and they noticed that the N400 evoked by incoming animate Agent arguments violating event knowledge (e.g. *The bass was strummed by **the drummer***) was strongly attenuated when they were semantically related to the context (e.g. *the drummer* is related to a *concert*-type scenario). In contrast, semantic relatedness did not modulate the N400 evoked by inanimate Agent arguments that violated the preceding verbs animacy selection restrictions (e.g. *The bass was strummed by **the drum***). Such a result led the researchers to the conclusion that the two types of violations are actually distinct at the brain processing level.

Moreover, Warren et al. (2015) recently brought new evidence that the violation of a selectional restriction determines higher processing complexity than simple event implausibility. In an eye-tracking experiment, the authors compared the reading times between sentences in three different experimental conditions: a plausible condition (i.e. *The hamster explored a backpack*), an implausible condition with no violation of selectional restrictions (*The hamster lifted a backpack*) and an impossible condition with violation (*The hamster entertained a backpack*). Although the difference in human possibility ratings was not statistically significant between the last two conditions, eye-movements evidenced longer disruption in the violation condition compared to the other two. They concluded suggesting that selectional restrictions could actually be coarse-grained semantic features, derived by means of abstractions over exemplar-type representations of events in memory. Violations of coarse-grained semantic features are likely to be detected earlier by the readers and cause more difficulty also in the later stages of processing, as they lead to such a degree of semantic anomaly that it becomes hard to build a coherent discourse model for the sentence (Warren and McConnell, 2007).

Most importantly, from a computational perspective, word combinations corresponding to the violations either of world knowledge (the implausible condition in Warren's data) or of selectional restrictions are not likely to be found in corpora of natural language data, and thus they cannot be distinguished on the basis of probabilistic methods. In our work we aim at testing the ability of thematic fit models to spot the difference and to assign different degrees of anomaly to the two conditions. The idea, intuitively, is that the degree of semantic anomaly goes hand in hand with an increase in processing complexity.

3 Experiments

For our experiments, we used two evaluation datasets: the sentences from the studies of Pylkkänen and McElree (2007) and Warren et al. (2015). The first study presented a magnetoencephalography experiment, with the goal of investigating the brain response to anomaly and to complement coercion, i.e. the case of a type clash between an event-selecting verb and an entity-denoting direct object. The experimental subjects were exposed to sentences in three different conditions: i) sentences with a typical verb-object combination (*The journalist wrote the article after his coffee break*); ii) sentences with a complement coercion (*The journalist began the article after his coffee break*); iii) sentences with a selectional restriction violation (*The journalist astonished the article after his coffee break*). This dataset is interesting for us because it will allow a direct comparison between violations of selectional restrictions and a similar phenomenon, the only difference being that a coercion involves the inference of a hidden verb (in the case of the example above, *writing*) that is not present in the linguistic input, leading to a sort of 'repair' of the violation. Discriminating between the two conditions is likely to be a difficult task.

The Warren dataset is the same of the study mentioned in Section 2.2. We are going to compare the items in the three conditions (plausible, implausible with no violation and impossible violation: see the examples in Section 2.2) of the experiment of Warren and colleagues, and we are particularly interested in the ability of the models to set the violation condition apart from the others. As declared by the authors themselves, they have built the sentences in a way than even the events described in the plausible condition are rare, or very unlikely. The test on this dataset will be particularly indicative of the performance of thematic fit models when they have to deal with different types of rare verb-argument combinations.

In both the datasets, we expect our thematic fit models to assign the lowest score to the violation condition, thus being able to distinguish between combinations that are simply unlikely and others that are really anomalous.

Datasets The Pylkkänen dataset is composed by 33 triplets of sentences, while the Warren dataset is composed by 30 triplets. We converted the experimental sentences in subject-verb-object triples. Here is one example from the Pylkkänen dataset (1) and one from the Warren dataset (2):

(1)   a.   *journalist-write-article* (typical)
        b.   *journalist-begin-article* (coercion)
        c.   *journalist-astonish-article* (violation)

(2)   a.   *hamster-explore-backpack* (plausible)
        b.   *hamster-lift-backpack* (implausible)
        c.   *hamster-entertain-backpack* (violation)

Before building our dependency-based DSM, we had to exclude three triplets from the Warren dataset since one or more words in the triplets had frequency below 100 in the training corpus. On the other hand, we have full coverage for the Pylkkänen dataset.

DSM We built a dependency-based DSM by using the data in the BNC corpus (Leech, 1992) and in the Wacky corpus (Baroni et al., 2009). Both the corpora were POS-tagged with the Tree Tagger (Schmid,

Verb and Role	Fillers
Agent of *to play*	actor, gamer, violinist
Agent of *to arrest*	cop, policeman, superhero
Patient of *to eat*	pizza, sandwich, ice-cream
Patient of *to shoot*	enemy, soldier, prey

Table 1: Verb roles and examples of fillers extracted by means of a corresponding syntactic relation.

1994) and parsed with the Maltparser (Nivre et al., 2006). [3] We extracted all the dependencies for the 20K most frequent words in the corpora, including the words of our datasets. Every co-occurrence between a target word and another context word in a given syntactic relation was weighted by means of Positive Local Mutual Information (Evert, 2004). [4] Given a target t, a relation r and a context word c occurring in the relation r with the target (e.g. $t = bark$, $r = sbj$, $c = dog$), we computed both their co-occurrence O_{trc}, and the expected co-occurrence E_{trc} under the assumption of statistical independence. The Positive Local Mutual Information (henceforth PLMI) is then computed as follows:

$$LMI(t, r, c) = log\left(\frac{O_{trc}}{E_{trc}}\right) * O_{trc} \tag{1}$$

$$PLMI(t, r, c) = max(LMI(t, r, c), 0) \tag{2}$$

Finally, each target word is represented by a vector of PLMI-weighted syntactic co-occurrences. Each contextual dimension corresponds to the co-occurrence of the target with a word in a given syntactic relation. For example, the vector of the verb *write-v* has dimensions such as *journalist-n:subj,article-n:obj* etc. [5]

Method As in Baroni and Lenci (2010), the thematic fit of a word for a given verb role is computed as the distributional similarity of that word with a *prototype representation* of the typical role filler. Such representation is obtained by averaging the vectors of the most typical fillers, i.e. words that are strongly associated with that verb-specific role. More concretely, the authors used syntactic functions to approximate thematic roles, and considered the most typical subjects of a verb as the fillers for the agent role, and the most typical objects as the fillers for the patient role. Typicality was measured by means of PLMI values: given a target verb t and a syntactic relation r, the typical fillers for the corresponding role were the 20 words with the highest PLMI association score with (t, r). Some examples of the extracted fillers are provided in Table 1. [6] Once built the prototype, the thematic fit of each candidate filler is assessed as the cosine similarity between the filler vector and the prototype itself.

For example, the prototype for the patient of *entertain-v* will be built out of the typical objects of the verb, such as *public, player* etc. Words that are distributionally similar to such fillers (i.e. *fan*) are likely to have a high thematic fit for the role.

Models In our experiments, we compared two different models of thematic fit. **B&L2010** is a 'classical' model of thematic fit, and it consists of a direct reimplementation of Baroni and Lenci (2010): since we are scoring sentences which differ for the degree of typicality of the verb-object combination, the scores assigned by this model will be the thematic fit scores θ of the object of each sentence given the verb and the patient role. In Equation 3, t is the target verb and c is a word occurring as an object (obj) of t:

$$\theta = \vec{c}\,|obj, \vec{t} \tag{3}$$

---

[3] We used the scripts of the DISSECT framework to build the distributional space (Dinu et al., 2013).

[4] As context words, we took into account only the 20K words of our target list, in order to limit the size of the distributional space.

[5] Obviously, including all the syntactic relations would have hugely increased the dimensionality of the vector space. Therefore, we took into account only the following relations: subject, direct and indirect object, prepositional complement. For each relation, we also considered its inverse: for example, the target *apple-v* has a dimension *eat-v:obj-1*, meaning that *apple* occurs as a direct object of *eat-v*.

[6] In the literature, 20 is a common choice for the number of fillers (Baroni and Lenci, 2010; Greenberg et al., 2015). Thus, we decided to keep this value for our experiments.

For example, the score of the sentence of the example 1a will be the thematic fit of the object *article-n* as a patient of *write-v*.

The second model is inspired by the proposal of Chersoni et al. (2016) who, instead of seeing the thematic fit as a simple measure of congruence between a predicate and an argument, considered it as a more general measure of the semantic coherence of an event. The global degree of semantic coherence is given by the product of the partial θ scores of all the event participants.

Similarly to Baroni and Lenci's model, each θ score is defined as the cosine similarity between an argument vector and the prototype vector for the slot, built as the centroid of its typical fillers. Once computed the partial θ scores, they are combined to find the global score θ_e.

$$\theta_e = \prod_{\vec{t},r,\vec{c} \in e} \theta(\vec{c}|r,\vec{t}) \tag{4}$$

where t is a target word in the event e [7], r is a syntactic relation and c is a context word occurring in the relation r with t (it is read as: the thematic fit score of c given the word t and the relation r).

For example, for the verb-argument triple of the example 1a, the three partial components of the final score would be: i) the thematic fit of the subject *journalist-n* as an agent of *write-v*; ii) the thematic fit of the object *article-n* as a patient of *write-v*; iii) the thematic fit of the object *article-n* as a co-argument of the subject *journalist-n*. [8]

The intuition of the authors was that the semantic coherence of an event does not depend simply on predicate-argument congruence scores, taken in isolation, but on a general degree of mutual typicality between all the participants. We will refer to this variant of the thematic fit model as **CBL2016**.

Task We evaluate the accuracy of the models in a classification task: for each triplet in the datasets, we compute the thematic fit scores for the subject-verb-object triples in the three conditions. We score a hit for a model each time it assigns the lowest score to the triple in the violation condition. The performance of both thematic fit models is compared to the one of a random baseline (since we have three different conditions, the accuracy is estimated to be 33.33%). We also use statistical tests to check in what measure the scores between the violation and the other conditions differ.

4   Results

The results of our experiments on the classification task are shown in Table 2 and Table 3. On the Warren dataset, the CBL2016 model performs extremely well, managing to assign the lowest thematic fit score to the violation condition in more than 80% of the triples of the dataset and reporting a highly significant advantage over the random baseline ($p < 0.001$) [9]. Although inferior in accuracy to the other model, B&L2010 manages as well to significantly outperform the baseline ($p < 0.05$). The Kruskal-Wallis test revealed a strong main effect of the condition on the scores assigned by both models (B&L2010: $\chi^2 = 20.502, p < 0.01$; CBL2016: $\chi^2 = 14.117, p < 0.01$). Post-hoc comparisons with the Wilcoxon rank sum test showed that, for both models, the scores differ significantly between the plausible and the violation condition and between the not plausible and the violation condition (in both cases, $p < 0.01$).

Model	Hits	Accuracy
Random	9/27	33.33%
B&L2010	18/27	66.66%
CBL2016	22/27	81.48%

Table 2: Accuracy scores for the Warren dataset.

---

[7] Keep in mind that, in the above-mentioned work, sentences are seen as linguistic descriptions of events and situations.

[8] The latter component was introduced because nouns, according to recent psycholinguistic studies (Hare et al., 2009; Bicknell et al., 2010), activate expectations about arguments typically co-occurring in the same events. In order to model the relationship between agents and patients of the same events, we introduced in our DSM the generic relation *verb* to link subjects and objects that tend to occur together, independently of the predicate.

[9] p-values computed with the χ^2 statistical test.

Model	Hits	Accuracy
Random	11/33	33.33%
B&L2010	21/33	63.63%
CBL2016	19/33	57.57%

Table 3: Accuracy scores for the Pylkkänen dataset.

These results are extremely relevant: although all the events of the Warren dataset have very low probabilities (for an explicit design choice of the authors), both the thematic models proved to be able to discriminate between events violating selectional restrictions and events that are simply unlikely (see also Figure 1, left side). They do not differ significantly for their ability to discriminate between the violation and the other conditions, as the violation consists of a mismatch of semantic features between the patient role of the verb and its filler (typically an animacy violation), and this information is available to both B&L2010 and CBL2016 in the form of an extremely low thematic fit for the patient. With respect to B&L2010, CBL2016 has also information on the thematic fit of the other event fillers. In theory, this should be an an advantage for distinguishing between the plausible and the not plausible condition: as it can be seen in Example 2, it is difficult to account for the difference in plausibility between a. and b. by only looking at the verb-patient combination. In practice, none of the models has assigned significantly different scores to the conditions a. and b., in line with the results of Warren et al. (2015), who also reported the absence of significant differences in reading times between plausible and not plausible sentences. This suggests that, for very rare events, different degrees of plausibility do not determine big changes in processing complexity, at least when selectional restrictions are not violated.

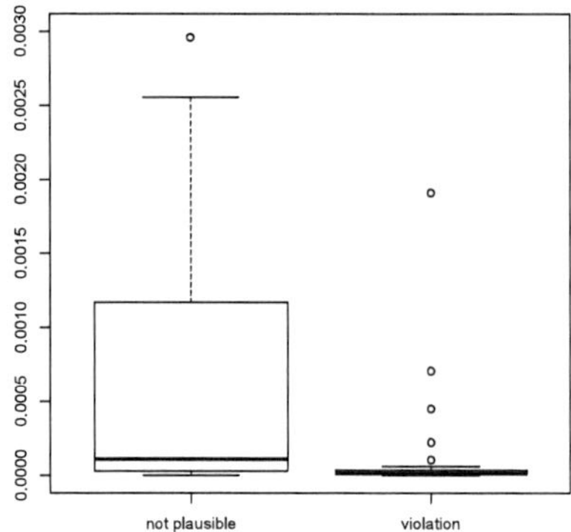
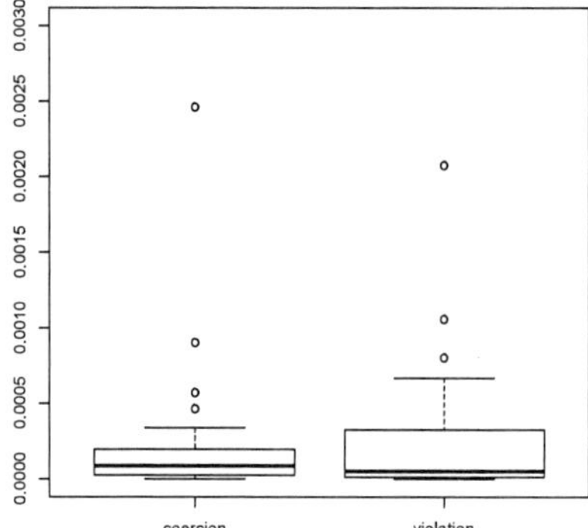

Figure 1: CBL 2016 score comparison between the NOT PLAUSIBLE and the VIOLATION condition on the Warren dataset (left) and between the COERCION and the VIOLATION condition on the Pylkkänen dataset (right).

As for the Pylkkänen dataset, both models were again able to outperform the random baseline on the classification task with a significant margin ($p < 0.05$) and, also on this dataset, the Kruskal-Wallis test showed a strong effect of the condition (B&L2010: $\chi^2 = 40.114$, $p < 0.001$; CBL2016: $\chi^2 = 13.804$, $p < 0.01$). The Wilcoxon test revealed that they are both efficient in discriminating between the typical and the other two conditions (B&L2010: $p < 0.001$ for both the typical-coercion and the typical-violation comparison; CBL2016: $p < 0.01$ for the same comparisons), but it revealed also an important difference: while B&L2010 assigns significantly higher scores to coerced sentences with respect to their counterparts containing violations ($p < 0.01$), CBL2016 fails to detect such a distinction ($p > 0.1$; see also Figure 1, right side). This result may seem surprising, since the less informed B&L2010 turns out to be the most efficient in detecting the fine-grained distinction between coercions and violations, simply on the basis of the typicality of the verb-patient argument combination.

A possible explanation is that the thematic fit was conceived in CBL2016 as a general index of semantic coherence. If we limit ourselves to compute the fit between the event and the participants that are present in the linguistic input, it is not surprising that coercions and violations have similarly low coherence levels. After all, coercions can be described as violations of selectional restrictions that are repaired by inferring a hidden verb from the context (e.g. *writing* in *The journalist began the article*): since the model has no way to infer the hidden verb, it assigns a similarly low coherence score to the two experimental conditions.

5   Conclusion

In this paper, we have evaluated two thematic fit models in a classification task for the identification of violations of selectional restrictions. Our models had to deal with extremely rare word combinations (in the case of the Warren dataset) or to distinguish between violations and a similar phenomenon, i.e. complement coercion (in the case of the Pylkkänen dataset). On the Warren data, the performance of both models was very solid, clearly showing that they are able to discriminate between unlikely and anomalous inputs. Typically, such rare verb-argument combinations are not attested at all in corpora. We think this is a proof that the role characterization in thematic fit models allows generalizations on potential fillers that go well beyond the observable evidence. On the Pylkkänen dataset, the classical model by Baroni and Lenci (2010) manages to distinguish between coercion and violation, whereas the more recent model by Chersoni et al. (2016) does not. Still, the predictions of the latter could find some justification in the rationale behind its notion of thematic fit, and in the particular nature of the coercion phenomenon, describable as an apparent violation that is repaired by inferring a covert event.

More in general, the notion of thematic fit turns out to be very useful for modeling processing complexity, measured as in the experimental studies (mostly) in terms of processing times. Since thematic fit quantifies how a given argument fits a given semantic role, or a given event scenario, the low values correspond to situations in which it is extremely difficult to build a coherent semantic representation for the sentence. Given these promising results, future research should aim at building larger datasets to evaluate distributional models on anomaly detection tasks.

Another issue that deserves further investigation is the effect of the general discourse context on event plausibility, since contextual information in the current datasets is often limited to the other argument fillers. [10] As shown by studies like Warren et al. (2008), a context such as a fantasy world scenario can modulate the plausibility of an event and consequently the processing times, and the same could be true also for some specific real world scenarios (i.e. a psychiatric hospital, a circus etc.). Future efforts in modeling semantic anomalies have to take into account the acquisitions of the rich experimental literature on the topic, and to try to integrate as many as possible types of contextual manipulation in building new gold standards.

Acknowledgements

This work has been carried out thanks to the support of the A*MIDEX grant (nANR-11-IDEX-0001-02) funded by the French Government "Investissements d'Avenir" program.

References

Marco Baroni, Silvia Bernardini, Adriano Ferraresi, and Eros Zanchetta. 2009. The WaCky Wide Web: A collection of Very Large Linguistically Processed Web-Crawled Corpora. In *Computational Linguistics*, 36(4): 673-721.

Marco Baroni and Alessandro Lenci. 2010. Distributional Memory: A General Framework for Corpus-based Semantics. In *Computational Linguistics*, 36(4): 673-721.

Klinton Bicknell, Jeffrey L Elman, Mary Hare, Ken McRae, and Marta Kutas. 2010. Effects of Event Knowledge in Processing Verbal Arguments. In *Journal of Memory and Language*, 63(4): 489-505.

Emmanuele Chersoni, Philippe Blache, and Alessandro Lenci. 2016. Towards a Distributional Model of Semantic Complexity. *Proceedings of the COLING Workshop on Computational Linguistics for Linguistic Complexity*.

---

[10]We thank one of the anonymous reviewers for pointing this out.

Georgiana Dinu, Nghia The Pham, and Marco Baroni. 2013. Dissect-Distributional Semantics Composition Toolkit. *Proceedings of ACL System Demonstrations*.

Katrin Erk, Sebastian Padó, and Ulrike Padó. 2010. A Flexible, Corpus-Driven Model of Regular and Inverse Selectional Preferences. In *Computational Linguistics*, 36(4): 723-763.

Todd Ferretti, Ken McRae, and Andrea Hatherell. 2001. Integrating Verbs, Situation Schemas, and Thematic Role Concepts. In *Journal of Memory and Language*, 44(4): 516-547.

Stefan Evert. 2004. The Statistics of Word Cooccurrences: Word Pairs and Collocations. PhD Thesis.

Jerry Fodor. 1983. The Modularity of Mind. MIT Press.

Clayton Greenberg, Asad Sayeed, and Vera Demberg. 2015. Improving Unsupervised Vector-Space Thematic Fit Evaluation via Role-Filler Prototype Clustering. *Proceedings of NAACL-HLT*.

Peter Hagoort, Lea Hald, Marcel Bastiaansen, and Karl Magnus Petersson. 2004. Integration of Word Meaning and World Knowledge in Language Comprehension. In *Science*, 304(5669), 438–441.

Mary Hare, Michael Jones, Caroline Thomson, Sarah Kelly, and Ken McRae. 2009. Reading Time Evidence for Enriched Composition. In *Cognition*, 111(2), 151–167.

Jerrold J Katz and Jerry Fodor. 1963. The Structure of a Semantic Theory. In *Language*, 39(2), 170–210.

Gina R Kuperberg. 2007. Neural Mechanisms of Language Comprehension: Challenges to syntax. In *Brain Research*, 1146, 23–49.

Gianluca E Lebani and Alessandro Lenci. 2018. A Distributional Model of Verb-Specific Semantic Roles Inferences. In *Language, Cognition, and Computational Models*, edited by Thierry Poibeau and Aline Villavicencio. Cambridge University Press.

Geoffrey Neil Leech. 1992. 100 Million Words of English: The British National Corpus (BNC).

Alessandro Lenci. 2008. Distributional Semantics in Linguistic and Cognitive Research. *Italian Journal of Linguistics*, 20(1), 1–31.

Alessandro Lenci. 2011. Composing and Updating Verb Argument Expectations: A Distributional Semantic Model. *Proceedings of the ACL Workshop on Cognitive Modeling and Computational Linguistics*.

Brian McElree, Matthew J Traxler, Martin J Pickering, Rachel E Seely, and Ray Jackendoff. 2001. Reading Time Evidence for Enriched Composition. In *Cognition*, 78(1), B17–B25.

Ken McRae, Micheal J Spivey-Knowlton, and Michael K Tanenhaus. 1998. Modeling the Influence of Thematic Fit (and Other Constraints) in Online Sentence Comprehension. In *Journal of Memory and Language*, 38(3), 283–312.

Ken McRae and Kazunaga Matsuki. 2009. People Use their Knowledge of Common Events to Understand Language, and Do So as Quickly as Possible. In *Language and Linguistics Compass*, 3(6), 1417–1429.

Mante S Nieuwland and Jos JA Van Berkum. 2006. When Peanuts Fall in Love: N400 Evidence for the Power of Discourse. In *Journal of Cognitive Neuroscience*, 18(7), 1098–1111.

Joakim Nivre, Johan Hall, and Jens Nilsson. 2006. Maltparser: A Data-Driven Parser-Generator for Dependency Parsing. *Proceedings of LREC*.

Martin Paczynski and Gina R Kuperberg. 2012. Multiple Influences of Semantic Memory on Sentence Processing: Distinct Effects of Semantic Relatedness on Violations of Real-World Event/State Knowledge and Animacy Selection Restrictions. In *Journal of Memory and Language*, 67(4), 426–448.

Ulrike Padó. 2007. The Integration of Syntax and Semantic Plausibility in a Wide-Coverage Model of Human Sentence Processing. PhD Thesis.

Liina Pylkkänen and Brian McElree. 2007. An MEG Study of Silent Meaning. In *Journal of Cognitive Neuroscience*, 19(11), 1905–1921.

Enrico Santus, Emmanuele Chersoni, Alessandro Lenci, and Philippe Blache. 2017. Measuring Thematic Fit with Distributional Feature Overlap. *Proceedings of EMNLP*.

Asad Sayeed and Vera Demberg. 2014. Combining Unsupervised Syntactic and Semantic Models of Thematic Fit. *Proceedings of CLIC.it.*

Asad Sayeed, Vera Demberg, and Pavel Shkadzko. 2014. An Exploration of Semantic Features in an Unsupervised Thematic Fit Evaluation Framework. In *Italian Journal of Computational Linguistics.*

Helmut Schmid. 1994. Part-of-Speech Tagging with Neural Networks. *Proceedings of COLING.*

Nathaniel J Smith and Roger Levy. 2013. The Effect of Word Predictability on Reading Time Is Logarithmic. In *Cognition*, 128(3), 302–319.

Matthew J Traxler, Martin J Pickering, and Brian McElree. 2002. Coercion in Sentence Processing: Evidence from Eye-Movements and Self-Paced Reading. In *Journal of Memory and Language*, 47(4), 530–547.

Eva Maria Vecchi, Marco Baroni, and Roberto Zamparelli. 2011. (Linear) Maps of the Impossible: Capturing Semantic Anomalies in Distributional Space. *Proceedings of the ACL Workshop on Distributional Semantics and Compositionality.*

Tessa Warren and Kerry McConnell. 2007. Investigating Effects of Selectional Restriction Violations and Plausibility Violation Severity on Eye-Movements in Reading. In *Psychonomic Bulletin and Review*, 14(4), 770–775.

Tessa Warren, Kerry McConnell and Keith Rayner. 2008. Effects of Context on Eye Movements when Reading about Possible and Impossible Events. In *Journal of Experimental Psychology*, 34(4).

Tessa Warren, Evelyn Milburn, Nikole D Patson, and Michael Walsh Dickey. 2015. Comprehending the Impossible: What Role Do Selectional Restriction Violations Play? In *Language, Cognition and Neuroscience*, 30(8), 932–939.

Alessandra Zarcone, Alessandro Lenci, Sebastian Padó, and Jason Utt. Fitting, not Clashing! A Distributional Semantic Model of Logical Metonymy. 2013. *Proceedings of IWCS.*

Comparing morphological complexity of Spanish, Otomi and Nahuatl

Ximena Gutierrez-Vasques
Universidad Nacional Autónoma
de México
Mexico City
xim@unam.mx

Victor Mijangos
Universidad Nacional Autónoma
de México
Mexico City
vmijangosc@ciencias.unam.mx

Abstract

We use two small parallel corpora for comparing the morphological complexity of Spanish, Otomi and Nahuatl. These are languages that belong to different linguistic families, the latter are low-resourced. We take into account two quantitative criteria, on one hand the distribution of types over tokens in a corpus, on the other, perplexity and entropy as indicators of word structure predictability. We show that a language can be complex in terms of how many different morphological word forms can produce, however, it may be less complex in terms of predictability of its internal structure of words.

1 Introduction

Morphology deals with the internal structure of words (Aronoff and Fudeman, 2011; Haspelmath and Sims, 2013). Languages of the world have different word production processes. Morphological richness vary from language to language, depending on their linguistic typology. In natural language processing (NLP), taking into account the morphological complexity inherent to each language could be important for improving or adapting the existing methods, since the amount of semantic and grammatical information encoded at the word level, may vary significantly from language to language.

Conceptualizing and quantifying linguistic complexity is not an easy task, many quantitative and qualitative dimensions must be taken into account (Miestamo, 2008). On one hand we can try to answer what is complexity in a language and which mechanisms express it, on the other hand, we can try to find out if there is a language with more complex phenomena (phonological, morphological, syntactical) than other and how can we measure it. Miestamo (2008) distinguishes between two types of complexity: the absolute, which defines complexity in terms of the number of parts of a system; and the relative, which is related to the cost and difficulty faced by language users. Some authors focuses in the absolute approach since it is less subjective. Another common complexity distinction is between global and particular. Global complexity characterizes entire languages, e.g., as easy or difficult to learn (Miestamo, 2008, p. 29), while particular complexity refers only to a level of the whole language (for example phonological complexity, morphological complexity, syntactical complexity).

We focus on morphological complexity. Many definitions of this term have been proposed (Baerman et al., 2015; Anderson, 2015; Sampson et al., 2009). From the computational linguistics perspective there has been a special interest in corpus based approaches to quantify it, i.e., methods that estimate the morphological complexity of a language directly from the production of morphological instances over a corpus. This type of approach usually represents a relatively easy and reproducible way to quantify complexity without the strict need of linguistic annotated data. The underlying intuition of corpus based methods is that morphological complexity depends on the morphological system of a language, like its inflectional and derivational processes. A very productive system will produce a lot of different word forms. This morphological richness can be captured with several statistical measures, e.g., information theory measures (Blevins, 2013) or type token relationships. For example, Bybee (2010, p. 9) affirms that "the token frequency of certain items in constructions [i.e., words] as well as the range of types [...] determines representation of the construction as well as its productivity".

Proceedings of the Workshop on Linguistic Complexity and Natural Language Processing, pages 30–37
Santa Fe, New Mexico, USA, August 25, 2018.

In this work, we are interested in using corpus based approaches; however, we would like to quantify the complexity not only by the type and token distributions over a corpus, but also by taking into account other important dimension: the predictability of a morph sequence (Montermini and Bonami, 2013). This is a preliminary work that takes as a case of study the distant languages Otomi, Nahuatl and Spanish. The general idea is to use parallel corpora, type-token relationship and some NLP strategies for measuring the predictability in statistical language models.

Additionally, most of the previous works do not analyze how the complexity changes when different types of morphological normalization procedures are applied to a language, e.g., lemmatization, stemming, morphological segmentation. This information could be useful for linguistic analysis and for measuring the impact of different word form normalization tools depending of the language. In this work, we analyze how the type-token relationship changes using different types of morphological normalization techniques.

1.1 The type-token relationship (TTR)

The type-token relationship (TTR) is the relationship that exists between the number of distinct words (types) and the total word count (tokens) within a text. This measure has been used for several purposes, e.g., as an indicator of vocabulary richness and style of an author (Herdan, 1966; Stamatatos, 2009), information flow of a text (Altmann and Altmann, 2008) and it has also been used in child language acquisition, psychiatry and literary studies (Malvern and Richards, 2002; Kao and Jurafsky, 2012).

TTR has proven to be a simple, yet effective, way to quantify the morphological complexity of a language. This is why it has been used to estimate morphological complexity using relatively small corpora (Kettunen, 2014). It has also shown a high correlation with other types of complexity measures like entropy and paradigm-based approaches that are based on typological information databases (Bentz et al., 2016)

It is important to notice that the value of TTR is affected by the type and length of the texts. However, one natural way to make TTRs comparable between languages is to use a parallel corpus, since the same meaning and functions are, more or less, expressed in the two languages. When TTR is measured over a parallel corpus, it provides a useful way to compare typological and morphological characteristics of languages. Kelih (2010) works with parallel texts of the Slavic language family to analyze morphological and typological features of the languages, i.e., he uses TTR for comparing the morphological productivity and the degree of syntheticity and analycity between the languages. Along the same line, Mayer et al. (2014) automatically extract typological features of the languages, e.g., morphological synthesis degree, by using TTR.

There exist several models that have been developed to examine the relationship between the types and tokens within a text (Mitchell, 2015). The most common one is the ratio $\frac{types}{tokens}$ and it is the one that we use in this work.

1.2 Entropy and Perplexity

In NLP, statistical language models are a useful tool for calculating the probability of any sequence of words in a language. These models need a corpus as training data, they are usually based on n-grams, and more recently, in neural representations of words.

Information theory based measures can be used to estimate the predictiveness of these models, i.e., perplexity and entropy. Perplexity is a common measure for the complexity of n-grams models in NLP (Brown et al., 1992). Perplexity is based in Shannon's entropy (Shannon et al., 1951) as the perplexity of a model μ is defined by the equation $2^{H(\mu)}$, where $H(\mu)$ es the entropy of the model (or random variable). Shannon's entropy had been used for measuring complexity of different systems. In linguistics, entropy is commonly used to measure the complexity of morphological systems (Blevins, 2013; Ackerman and Malouf, 2013; Baerman, 2012). Higher values of perplexity and entropy mean less predictability.

Perplexity depends on how the model is represented (this includes the size of the data). In this work, we compare two different models for calculating the entropy and perplexity: a typical bigram model adapted to a morph level(Brown et al., 1992); and our proposal based on using the word as a context instead of ngrams.

We rely in parallel corpora to compare the measures across languages, since the same meaning and functions are shared in the two languages.

Bigram model. This model takes into consideration bigrams (Brown et al., 1992) as context for determining the joint probabilities of the sub-strings. Here the bigrams are sequences of two morphs in the text (whether they belong to the same word or not). This is a typical statistical language model but instead of using sequences of words, we use morphological segmented texts. In addition, we use a Laplacian (or add one) smoothing for the conditional probabilities (Chen and Goodman, 1999).

Word level. The word level representation takes the whole word as context for the determination of joint probabilities. Therefore, the frequency of co-occurrence is different from zero only if the sub-word units (morphs) are part of the same word. For example, if xby is a word with a prefix x and a suffix y, the co-occurrence of x with b will be different from zero as both morphs are part of the word xby. Similarly, the co-occurrence of y with b will be different from zero. Conversely, if two morphs are sub-strings of different words, its co-occurrence will be zero. To calculate the conditional probabilities we use and add one estimator defined as:

$$p(x|y) = \frac{fr(x, y) + 1}{fr(x, y) + V} \tag{1}$$

Where V is the number of types and $fr(\cdot)$ is the frequency of co-occurrence function.

2 Experimental setting

2.1 The corpus

We work with two language pairs that are spoken in the same country (Mexico) but they are typologically distant languages: Spanish (Indo-European)-Nahuatl (Uto-Aztecan) and Spanish-Otomi (Oto-Manguean). Both, Nahuatl and Otomi are low-resource languages that face scarcity of digital parallel and monolingual corpora.

Nahuatl is an indigenous language with agglutinative and polysynthethic morphological phenomena. It can agglutinate many different prefixes and suffixes to build complex words. Spanish also has rich morphology, but it mainly uses suffixes and it can have a fusional behavior, where morphemes can be fused or overlaid into a single one that encodes several grammatical meanings. Regarding to Otomi, its morphology also has a fusional tendency, and it is head-marking. Otomi morphology is usually considered quite complex (Palancar, 2012) as it exhibits different phenomena like stem alternation, inflectional class changes and suprasegmental variation, just to mention some.

Since we are dealing with low resource languages that have a lot of dialectal and orthographic variation, it is difficult to obtain a standard big parallel corpus. We work with two different parallel corpora, i.e., Spanish-Nahuatl and Spanish-Otomi. Therefore the complexity comparisons are always in reference to Spanish.

We used a Spanish-Nahuatl parallel corpus created by Gutierrez-Vasques et al. (2016). However, we used only a subset since the whole corpus is not homogeneous, i.e., it comprises several Nahuatl dialects, sources, periods of time and it lacks of a general orthographic normalization. We chose the texts that had a more or less systematic writing. On the other hand, we used a Spanish-Otomi parallel corpus (Lastra, 1992) conformed by 38 texts transcribed from speech. This corpus was obtained in San Andrés Cuexcontitlan. It is principally composed by narrative texts, but also counts with dialogues and elicited data. Table 1 shows the size of the parallel corpora used for the experiments.

2.2 Morphological analysis tools

We used different morphological analysis tools, in order to explore the morphological complexity variation among languages and between the different types of morphological representations. We performed lemmatization for Spanish language, and morphological segmentation for all languages.

Parallel Corpus	Tokens	Types
Spanish-Nahuatl		
Spanish (ES)	118364	13233
Nahuatl (NA)	81850	21207
Spanish-Otomi		
Spanish (ES)	8267	2516
Otomi (OT)	6791	3381

Table 1: Size of the parallel corpus

In NLP, morphology is usually tackled by building morphological analysis (taggers) tools. And more commonly, lemmatization and stemming methods are used to reduce the morphological variation by converting words forms to a standard form, i.e., a lemma or a stem. However, most of these technologies are focused in a reduced set of languages. For languages like English, with plenty of resources and relatively poor morphology, morphological processing may be considered solved.

However, this is not the case for all the languages. Specially for languages with rich morphological phenomena where it is not enough to remove inflectional endings in order to obtain a stem.

Lemmatization and stemming aim to remove inflectional endings. Spanish has available tools to perform this task. We used the tool Freeling[1]. Regarding to morphological segmentation, we used semi-supervised statistical segmentation models obtained with the tool Morfessor (Virpioja et al., 2013). In particular, we used the same segmentation models reported in Gutierrez-Vasques (2017) for Spanish and Nahuatl. As for Otomi, we used manual morphological segmentation of the corpus, provided by a specialist.

2.3   Complexity measures

We calculated the type-token relationship for every language in each parallel corpus. Table 2 shows the TTR of the texts without any processing (ES, NA) and with the different types of morphological processing: morphological segmentation (ES_{morph}, NA_{morph}), lemmatization (ES_{lemma}). In a similar way, Table 3 shows the TTR values for the Spanish-Otomi corpus. It is worth mentioning that the TTR values are only comparable within the same parallel corpus.

	Tokens	Types	TTR (%)
ES	118364	13233	11.17
NA	81850	21207	**25.90**
ES_{morph}	189888	4369	2.30
NA_{morph}	175744	2191	**1.24**
ES_{lemma}	118364	7599	6.42

Table 2: TTR for Nahuatl-Spanish corpus

	Tokens	Types	TTR (%)
ES	8267	2516	30.43
OT	6791	3381	**49.78**
ES_{morph}	14422	1072	7.43
OT_{morph}	13895	1788	**1.28**
ES_{lemma}	8502	1020	8.33

Table 3: TTR for Otomi-Spanish corpus

We also calculate the perplexity and complexity for the different languages. Since we are focusing on morphological complexity, we took only the segmented data for computing the entropy and the perplexity. We do not use the lemmatized or non segmented data since this would be equivalent to measuring the combinatorial complexity between words, i.e. syntax. In this sense, the entropy and

---

[1] http://nlp.lsi.upc.edu/freeling/

perplexity reflects the predictability of the morphs sequences. Tables 4 and 5 shows the perplexity and entropy in each language pair.

	Word level	Bigram model
	ES-NA	
NA_{morph}	214.166	1069.973
ES_{morph}	1222.956	2089.774
	ES-OT	
ES_{morph}	208.582	855.1766
OT_{morph}	473.830	1315.006

Table 4: Perplexity obtained in the different parallel corpora

	Word level	Bigram model
	ES-NA	
NA_{morph}	0.697	0.906
ES_{morph}	0.848	0.911
	ES-OT	
ES_{morph}	0.765	0.967
OT_{morph}	0.843	0.984

Table 5: Entropy obtained in the different parallel corpora

3 Results analysis

3.1 TTR as a measure of morphological complexity

When no morphological processing is applied, Nahuatl has a lot higher TTR value than Spanish, i.e., a greater proportion of different word forms (types). In spite of Nahuatl having fewer tokens because of its agglutinative nature, it has a lot more types than Spanish. This suggests that Nahuatl has a highly productive system that can generate a great number of different morphological forms. In other words, it is more likely to find a repeated word in Spanish than in a Nahuatl corpus. In the case of Otomi-Spanish, Otomi also has a bigger complexity compared to Spanish in terms of TTR. Even though both Otomi and Spanish show fusional patterns in its inflection, Otomi also count with a lot of derivational processes and shows regular stem alternations.

In every case, morphological segmentation induced the smallest values of TTR for all languages. Suggesting that greater reduction of the morphological complexity is achieved when the words are split into morphs, making it more likely to find a repeated item. For instance, when Nahuatl was morphologically segmented, TTR had a dramatic decrease (from 26.22 to 1.23). This TTR reduction could be the result of eliminating the combinatorial variety of the agglutinative and polysynthetical morphology of the language. Therefore, when we segment the text we break this agglutination, leading to significantly less diverse units.

In the case of Otomi language, a similar trend can be observed. Otomi seems to be morphologically more complex than Spanish in terms of TTR, i.e., more diverse types or word forms. When morphological segmentation is applied, TTR decreases and Otomi language has a lower TTR compared to Spanish. Even though Otomi is not a polysynthetic language like Nahuatl, these results suggest that Otomi has also a great combinatory potential of its morphs, i.e, when Otomi gets morphologically segmented we obtain less diverse types, these morphs may be recurrent in the text but they can be combined in many several ways within the Otomi word structure. Linguistic studies have shown that Otomi language can concatenate several affixes, specially in derivative processes (Lastra, 1992).

It has brought to our attention that Spanish has a higher TTR than Nahuatl and Otomi, only when the languages are morphologically segmented. It seems that the morphs inventory is bigger in Spanish, we conjecture this is related to the fact that Spanish has more suppletion or "irregular" forms phenomena (Boyé and Hofherr, 2006).

3.2 Predictability

The predictability of the internal structure of word is other dimension of complexity. It reflects the difficulty of producing novel words given a set of lexical items (stems, suffixes or morphs). First of all, as a general overview, we can see that word level models have the lower perplexity and entropy (Tables 4 and 5). We believe that this type of models capture better the morphological structure, since they take into account the possible combinations of morphs within a word and not outside the bounds of it (like the bigram model).

It is interesting to compare the TTR and the predictability measures for each language. In the case of Nahuatl, TTR shows that there is a lot of complexity at lexical level (many different word forms, few repetitions), however, this contrasts with the predictability of the elements that conform a lexical item: the combination of morphs within a word is more predictable than Spanish, since it obtains lower values of Perplexity and entropy. The combinatorial structure of Nahuatl morphology shows less uncertainty than Spanish one, despite the fact that Nahuatl is capable of producing many more different types in the corpus due to its agglutinative and polysynthetic nature.

The case of Otomi language is different, since it seems that it is not only complex in terms of TTR but also in terms of predictability. It obtains higher entropy and perplexity than Spanish. We conjecture this is related to several phenomena. For instance, Otomi and Nahuatl allow a large number of morphs combinations to modify a stem (inflectional and derivational). However, Otomi shows phenomena that is not easy to predict; for example, it has a complex system of inflectional classes, stem alternations and prefix changes. Moreover, tones and prosody plays an important role in the morphology of Otomi verbs (Palancar, 2004; Palancar, 2016). Also, we mentioned before that many of the affixes concatenations in Otomi take place in derivative processes. Derivation tends to be less predictable than inflection phenomena (derivation is less frequent and less regular), and this could be an additional reason of why the entropy values of this language are high.

4   Conclusions

In this work we used corpus based measures like TTR, entropy and perplexity for exploring the morphological complexity of three languages, using two small parallel corpora. We use TTR as a measure of morphological productivity of a language, and we use the entropy and perplexity calculated over a sequence of morphs, as a measure of predictability.

There may be a common believe that polysynthetical languages are far more complex than analytic ones. However, it is important to take into account the many factors that lay a role in the complexity of the system. We stressed out that morphological complexity has several dimensions that must be taken into account (Baerman et al., 2015).

While some agglutinative polysynthetical languages, like Nahuatl, could be considered complex by the number of morphemes the combinations and the information than can be encoded in a single word; the sequence of these elements may be more predictable than fusional languages like Spanish.

Languages like Otomi, showed high complexity in the two dimensions that we focused in this work (this is consistent with qualitative perspectives (Palancar, 2016)).

These two dimensions of complexity are valid and complementary. Measures like TTR reflect the amount of information that words can encode in a language, languages that have a high TTR have the potential of encoding a lot of functions at the word level, therefore, they produce many different word forms. Perplexity and entropy measured over a sequence of morphs reflect the predictability or degree of uncertainty of these combinations. The higher the entropy (hence, the perplexity), the higher the uncertainty in the combinations of morphs.

This was a preliminary work. Deeper linguistic analysis, more corpora and more languages are needed. However, we believe that quantitative measures extracted from parallel corpora can complement and deepen the study of linguistic complexity. Efforts are currently being made (Bane, 2008). However, more studies are needed, especially for low resources languages.

4.1 Future work

Languages of the world have a wide range of functions that can be codified at the world level. Therefore, it would be interesting to consider the study of more complexity dimensions in our work. Popular quantitative approaches are successful in reflecting how many morphs can be combined into a single word. However, it is also important to take into account how complex the format of a word can be, i.e., not only how many elements can be combined but also what type of elements. For example, Dahl (2009) argues that when a phoneme is added to a word, this process is not as complex as adding a tone.

Another interesting dimension is the complexity of the morphology in terms of acquisition (of native and L2 speakers). Miestamo (2008) points out that this typo of complexity should be made on the basis of psycho-linguistics analysis in both processing and acquisition.

Finally, one important factor that influences language complexity is culture. In many languages, pragmatics nuances are produced via morphological processes. For instance, languages like Nahuatl have a complex honorific or reverential system that is expressed using different types of affixes. Spanish expresses this type of phenomena with morphosyntactic processes. It is a challenging task to be able to quantify all these factors that play a role in the complexity of a language.

Acknowledgements

This work was supported by the Mexican Council of Science and Technology (CONACYT), fund 2016-01-2225, and CB-2016/408885. We also thank the reviewers for their valuable comments and to our friend Morrisé P. Martinez for his unconditional support.

References

Farrell Ackerman and Robert Malouf. 2013. Morphological organization: The low conditional entropy conjecture. *Language*, 89(3):429–464.

Vivien Altmann and Gabriel Altmann. 2008. Anleitung zu quantitativen textanalysen. *Methoden und Anwendungen*.

Stephen R Anderson. 2015. Dimensions of morphological complexity. *Understanding and measuring morphological complexity*, pages 11–26.

Mark Aronoff and Kirsten Fudeman. 2011. *What is morphology?*, volume 8. John Wiley & Sons.

Matthew Baerman, Dunstan Brown, and Greville G Corbett. 2015. *Understanding and measuring morphological complexity*. Oxford University Press, USA.

Matthew Baerman. 2012. Paradigmatic chaos in nuer. *Language*, 88(3):467–494.

Max Bane. 2008. Quantifying and measuring morphological complexity. In *Proceedings of the 26th west coast conference on formal linguistics*, pages 69–76. Somerville, MA, USA: Cascadilla Proceedings Project.

Christian Bentz, Tatjana Soldatova, Alexander Koplenig, and Tanja Samardžić. 2016. A comparison between morphological complexity measures: typological data vs. language corpora.

James P Blevins. 2013. The information-theoretic turn. *Psihologija*, 46(4):355–375.

Gilles Boyé and Patricia Hofherr. 2006. The structure of allomorphy in spanish verbal inflection. *Cuadernos de Lingüística del Instituto Universitario Ortega y Gasset*, 13:9–24.

Peter F Brown, Peter V Desouza, Robert L Mercer, Vincent J Della Pietra, and Jenifer C Lai. 1992. Class-based n-gram models of natural language. *Computational linguistics*, 18(4):467–479.

Joan Bybee. 2010. *Language, usage and cognition*. Cambridge University Press.

Stanley F Chen and Joshua Goodman. 1999. An empirical study of smoothing techniques for language modeling. *Computer Speech & Language*, 13(4):359–394.

Östen Dahl. 2009. *Testing the assumption of complexity invariance: The case of Elfdalian and Swedish*. na.

Ximena Gutierrez-Vasques, Gerardo Sierra, and Isaac Hernandez Pompa. 2016. Axolotl: a web accessible parallel corpus for spanish-nahuatl. In *Proceedings of the Tenth International Conference on Language Resources and Evaluation (LREC 2016)*.

Ximena Gutierrez-Vasques. 2017. Exploring bilingual lexicon extraction for Spanish-Nahuatl. In *ACL Workshop in Women and Underrepresenting Minorities in Natural Language Processing*.

Martin Haspelmath and Andrea Sims. 2013. *Understanding morphology*. Routledge.

Gustav Herdan. 1966. *The advanced theory of language as choice and chance*. Springer-Verlag New York.

Justine Kao and Dan Jurafsky. 2012. A computational analysis of style, affect, and imagery in contemporary poetry. In *Proceedings of the NAACL-HLT 2012 Workshop on Computational Linguistics for Literature*, pages 8–17.

Emmerich Kelih. 2010. The type-token relationship in slavic parallel texts. *Glottometrics*, 20:1–11.

Kimmo Kettunen. 2014. Can type-token ratio be used to show morphological complexity of languages? *Journal of Quantitative Linguistics*, 21(3):223–245.

Yolanda Lastra. 1992. *El otomí de Toluca*. IIA, UNAM.

David Malvern and Brian Richards. 2002. Investigating accommodation in language proficiency interviews using a new measure of lexical diversity. *Language testing*, 19(1):85–104.

Thomas Mayer, Bernhard Wälchli, Christian Rohrdantz, and Michael Hund. 2014. From the extraction of continuous features in parallel texts to visual analytics of heterogeneous areal-typological datasets. *Language Processing and Grammars. The role of functionally oriented computational models*, pages 13–38.

Matti Miestamo. 2008. Grammatical complexity in a cross-linguistic perspective. *Language complexity: Typology, contact, change*, pages 23–41.

David Mitchell. 2015. Type-token models: a comparative study. *Journal of Quantitative Linguistics*, 22(1):1–21.

Fabio Montermini and Olivier Bonami. 2013. Stem spaces and predictability in verbal inflection. *Lingue e linguaggio*, 12(2):171–190.

Enrique L Palancar. 2004. Verbal morphology and prosody in otomi. *International journal of American linguistics*, 70(3):251–278.

Enrique L Palancar. 2012. The conjugation classes of tilapa otomi: An approach from canonical typology.

Enrique L Palancar. 2016. A typology of tone and inflection: A view from the oto-manguean languages of mexico. *Tone and inflection: New facts and new perspectives*, pages 109–139.

Geoffrey Sampson, David Gil, and Peter Trudgill. 2009. *Language complexity as an evolving variable*, volume 13. Oxford University Press.

Claude E Shannon, Warren Weaver, and Arthur W Burks. 1951. The mathematical theory of communication.

Efstathios Stamatatos. 2009. A survey of modern authorship attribution methods. *Journal of the American Society for information Science and Technology*, 60(3):538–556.

Sami Virpioja, Peter Smit, Stig-Arne Grönroos, Mikko Kurimo, et al. 2013. Morfessor 2.0: Python implementation and extensions for morfessor baseline.

Uniform Information Density Effects on Syntactic Choice in Hindi

Ayush Jain
USC

Vishal Singh
NYU

Sidharth Ranjan
IIT Delhi

ayushj240,vishal.singh5846,sidharth.ranjan03@gmail.com

Rajakrishnan Rajkumar
IISER Bhopal
rajak@iiserb.ac.in

Sumeet Agarwal
IIT Delhi
sumeet@iitd.ac.in

Abstract

According to the UNIFORM INFORMATION DENSITY (UID) hypothesis (Levy and Jaeger, 2007; Jaeger, 2010), speakers tend to distribute information density across the signal uniformly while producing language. The prior works cited above studied syntactic reduction in language production at *particular choice points* in a sentence. In contrast, we use a variant of the above UID hypothesis in order to investigate the extent to which word order choices in Hindi are influenced by the drive to minimize the variance of information across *entire sentences*. To this end, we propose multiple lexical and syntactic measures (at both word and constituent levels) to capture the uniform spread of information across a sentence. Subsequently, we incorporate these measures in machine learning models aimed to distinguish between a naturally occurring corpus sentence and its grammatical variants (expressing the same idea). Our results indicate that our UID measures are not a significant factor in predicting the corpus sentence in the presence of lexical surprisal, a competing control predictor. Finally, in the light of other recent works, we conclude with a discussion of reasons for UID not being suitable for a theory of word order.

1 Introduction

The Uniform Information Density (henceforth UID) hypothesis states that language production exhibits a preference for distributing information uniformly across a linguistic signal. This hypothesis has a long history in the literature and Ferrer-i-Cancho (2017) traces the idea to the pioneering work of August and Gertraud Fenk (Fenk and Fenk-Oczlon, 1980) and developed further in subsequent articles (Fenk-Oczlon, 2001, for an overview). In recent years, this hypothesis has gained substantial traction with the work on syntactic reduction done by Florian Jaeger and colleagues (Levy and Jaeger, 2007; Jaeger, 2010). They show that speakers achieve uniformity of information across utterances either by omitting optional function words (like the *that* complementizer) or by explicitly mentioning them. In contrast to the two prior works cited above, which look at information density at *particular choice points* in language production, we examine a variant of the UID hypothesis stated above in the case of *entire sentences* created by syntactic alternations.

In this work, we test the hypothesis that reference sentences obtained from a corpus of naturally occurring written text exhibit greater uniformity in the spread of information in comparison to grammatical variants expressing the same idea. To this end, inspired from Collins (2014), we propose five distinct UID measures quantifying the uniformity of information density at both syntactic and lexical levels. We test two different versions of these measures at word as well as constituent boundaries. We examine the impact our UID measures in predicting syntactic choice in Hindi, an Indo-Aryan language with predominantly SOV word order and case-marking postpositions. This is the first work on the Hindi language (to the best of our knowledge), which studies its information-theoretic properties pertaining to syntac-

The first three authors listed are joint first authors. Ayush Jain and Vishal Singh undertook this project while they were undergraduate students at IIT Delhi.

Proceedings of the Workshop on Linguistic Complexity and Natural Language Processing, pages 38–48
Santa Fe, New Mexico, USA, August 25, 2018.

tic choice. In comparison to English (SVO order and prepositions), Hindi has relatively flexible word order (Agnihotri, 2007; Kachru, 2006).

Our study uses written data from the Hindi-Urdu Treebank (HUTB) corpus (Bhatt et al., 2009) consisting of newswire text. Hence the sentences used in our study are by default set in a given context. In addition to production ease, the language production system also factors in communicative considerations pertaining to facilitating comprehension for listeners (i.e. *audience design*) and for the speakers themselves (Jaeger and Buz, in press). Moreover, written text is often edited, taking into account comprehensibility considerations explicitly[1]. From the perspective of online language comprehension, processing difficulty is quantified by surprisal (Hale, 2001; Levy, 2008). We examine whether the UID measures we defined are significant predictors of syntactic choice even amidst lexical and syntactic surprisal as control factors (modelling comprehension considerations). Our experiments primarily involved the task of classifying Hindi data into reference sentences and artificial generated variants created by linearizing dependency trees corresponding to reference sentences in the HUTB corpus. Our UID measures were deployed as features in machine learning models to perform this binary classification task.

Our results indicate that logistic regression models containing lexical surprisal along with our lexical and syntactic UID measures (across words as well as constituents) do not significantly outperform a strong baseline model containing only lexical surprisal (estimated using a simple trigram model over words). Weak effects of both lexical and syntactic UID measures are attested in some non-canonical word order sequences involving object fronting. However, these are not in the expected direction *i.e.*, corpus sentences are characterized by spikes and troughs in information across words compared to their artificially generated variants. This result is very similar to that reported in the work of (Maurits et al., 2010), where the authors showed that object-first orders are in conflict with their formulation of the UID hypothesis. Using a corpus study as well as results from judgement tasks, they show that such orders cause troughs in the signal compared to other orders because of the disproportionate amount of information clustered around the object, making subsequent elements of the sentence redundant. They also point out the failure of their version of the UID hypothesis in the case of SOV languages. They attribute it to the presence of other stronger factors in such languages. On a related note, Ferrer-i-Cancho (2017) discuss how predicting the final verb is a stronger processing pressure in verb-final languages compared to other competing principles like dependency length minimization. Our result demonstrating lexical surprisal as a robust predictor of Hindi syntactic choice, adds support to predictability as a strong determinant of syntactic choice. Thus we conclude that the UID hypothesis (as defined by our measures) does not shape word order choices in Hindi when other control factors like predictability are considered. We discuss possible reasons for this by alluding to the work of (Ferrer-i-Cancho, 2017). This recent work suggests that UID might not be appropriate for a theory of word order of languages and UID might be restricted to account for syntactic reduction phenomena only.

The paper is structured as follows. Section 2 offers a brief background on the UID hypothesis and surprisal. Section 3 describes the UID measures we proposed as part of this work. Section 4 provides details of the datasets and models we used for testing our hypotheses. Section 5 presents the experiments conducted as part of the study and Section 6 discusses the implications of the results obtained for a theory of word order. Finally, Section 7 summarizes the conclusions as well as reflects on possible directions of future inquiry.

2 Background

The UNIFORM INFORMATION DENSITY principle discussed by (Jaeger, 2010) predicts that language production is optimized to distribute information uniformly across the utterance without exceeding the capacity of the communication channel. Claude Shannon's definition of information (Shannon, 1948) is adopted in this work. Information is defined as the negative log of the conditional probability of the linguistic unit (usually a word) in a given context. In context of omission or mention of the optional *that*-complementizer in English, Jaeger hypothesized that if the information density at the beginning

---

[1]In early Natural Language Generation research, editing performed by authors was considered to be akin to the self-monitoring component in Willem Levelt's 1989 model of human language production (Neumann and van Noord, 1992).

of a complement clause (CC) is high enough to exceed the capacity of the communication channel, then native speakers tend to explicity mention the *that*-complementizer at the start of the complement clause. The reason for this is the impact of the high frequency word *that* in reducing the information density at the CC onset. Conversely, for a CC with low information density at the beginning, omitting the *that*-complementizer would achieve the effect of increasing the information density at this choice point. Jaeger tested this hypothesis by examining *that*-reduction in the Switchboard corpus of English conversational speech. This study conclusively showed that information density is a significant predictor of *that*-mention (or omission) even while controls based on competing hypotheses were included in the statistical model to predict complementizer choice in spoken English.

Surprisal is mathematically equivalent to information density defined for language production, but it is an indicator of human sentence comprehension load based on different theoretical assumptions about activation allocation (Hale, 2001; Levy, 2008). We use two standard definitions of surprisal in this work as described below:

1. **Lexical surprisal** for word $k+1$ is defined using the conditional probability of a word given its two word sentential context and estimated using a simple trigram model over words. Mathematically, surprisal of the $(k+1)^{th}$ word, w, $S_{k+1} = -\log P(w_{k+1}|w_{k-1}, w_k)$.

2. **Syntactic surprisal** is computed using the probabilistic incremental dependency parser developed by (Agrawal et al., 2017), which is based on the parallel-processing variant of the *arc-eager* parsing strategy (Nivre, 2008) proposed by (Boston et al., 2011). This parser maintains a set of the most probable parses at each word as it proceeds through the sentence. A maximum-entropy classifier is used to estimate the probability of a transition from one parser state to the next, and the probability of a parser state is taken to be the product of the probabilities of all transitions made to reach that state. The syntactic surprisal of the $(k+1)^{th}$ word is computed as the log-ratio of the sum of probabilities of maintained parser states at word k to the same sum at word $k+1$.

3 UID Measures

This section describes in detail the five distinct UID measures (two normalized and three unnormalized) we propose as part of this work, in accordance to our version of the UID hypothesis pertaining to entire sentences (as opposed to particular choice points in Jaeger's work). The unnormalized measures are along the lines of UID measures proposed in (Collins, 2014) and their normalized counterparts are our own original contribution. In our work, contextual probabilities used to quantify information density were estimated using lexical as well as syntactic surprisal models described in the previous section. Notation: N is the number of words in a sentence, id_i is the information density (negative lexical/syntactic log-prob) of the ith word of the sentence and μ is defined as the mean information density of the sentence, i.e., $\mu \equiv \frac{1}{N} \sum_{i=1}^{N} id_i$.

1. **Global UID Measure**: $UIDglob = -\frac{1}{N} \sum_{i=1}^{N} (id_i - \mu)^2$

   This measure encapsulates the negative **variance** of information present in a sentence. This is the crux of UID hypothesis which states that the information content at different points in a sentence should not vary much. Thus negative variance appears to be the most straightforward way to capture the uniformity in information density in the sentence.

2. **Local UID Measure**: $UIDloc = -\frac{1}{N} \sum_{i=2}^{N} (id_i - id_{i-1})^2$

   This score represents the negative mean-squared increase or decrease of information content per word, relative to the preceding word. This measure looks at the local uniformity in information in comparison to $UIDglob$ which looks at the global uniformity of the sentence.

3. **Normalized Global UID Measure**: $UIDglobNorm = -\frac{1}{N} \sum_{i=1}^{N} (\frac{id_i}{\mu} - 1)^2$

   It seems natural to judge the extent of variance in the information density as a fraction of the mean value for a given sentence, rather than in absolute terms. So we normalize the UID measure by the mean of the n-gram information density over all the words in the sentence (μ), to get a measure of (negative) variance relative to the mean.

Predictor(s)	Word-based UID measures				Constituent-based UID measures			
	Lexical		Syntactic		Lexical		Syntactic	
	Weight(s)	%Acc	Weight(s)	%Acc	Weight(s)	%Acc	Weight(s)	%Acc
UIDglob	1.08	72.19	0.40	52.43	-0.88	65.54	-0.02	51.61
UIDloc	0.89	71.22	0.02	49.94	-0.6	53.83	0.08	50.71
UIDglobNorm	-13.11	73.05	-0.09	53.16	-0.81	80.06	0.23	52.81
UIDlocNorm	-2.34	62.38	-0.15	53.9	-0.81	69.76	0.11	53.87
UIDlocPrevNorm	0.00	51.23	0.00	53.58	0.005	39.4	0.00	51.87
Surprisal	-0.81	89.96	-0.11	56.48	-0.81	89.95	-0.11	56.38
Lexical surprisal+UIDglob	-1.00, -0.42	89.99	-0.81, 0.01	89.96	-0.79, -0.18	90.08	-0.74, 0.00	89.96
Lexical surprisal+UIDloc	-0.97, -0.11	90.01	-0.95, 0.04	89.97	-0.80, -0.04	90.00	-0.98, 0.07	90.01
Lexical surprisal+UIDglobNorm	-0.96, -2.18	89.98	-0.81, -0.01	89.96	-0.91, -3.75	90.12	-0.93, 0.13	89.99
Lexical surprisal+UIDlocNorm	-0.98, -0.68	89.99	-0.81, -0.02	89.95	-0.96, -0.50	90.00	-0.74, 0.05	89.98

Table 1: Classification performance of various word and constituent-based UID measures

4. **Normalized Local UID Measure**: $UIDlocNorm = -\frac{1}{N}\frac{\sum_{i=2}^{N}(id_i - id_{i-1})^2}{\mu^2}$

   This measure similarly normalises $UIDloc$ using the mean information density of the sentence.

5. **Previous Word Normalized Local UID Measure**: $UIDlocPrevNorm = -\frac{1}{N}\sum_{i=2}^{N}\left(\frac{id_i}{id_{i-1}} - 1\right)^2$

   Here the normalisation is local as well: with respect to the information density of just the preceding word, rather than the mean for the complete sentence. $UIDlocPrevNorm$ is essentially the negation of the mean-squared fractional deviation in information as one traverses the sentence from one word to the next.

4 Data and Models

This section describes the datasets and models we used to test our hypotheses on Hindi. For this study, a total of 8736 labelled, projective dependency trees from the Hindi-Urdu Treebank (HUTB) corpus of written Hindi (Bhatt et al., 2009) were used in our experiments. Variants were generated for each of these trees by randomly permuting preverbal constituents (in the preverbal domain itself). A set of non-corpus variants was creating by randomly choosing utmost 99 such variants corresponding to each HUTB reference sentence. Subsequently, from this set of variants, we filtered out variants containing preverbal dependency relation sequences not attested in the HUTB. This was done as a mechanism to automatically ensure that very unacceptable variants were eliminated from our study. We would like to note that this filtering is not crucial to our results in any way. An earlier unfiltered dataset consisting of all variants also showed similar trends in the results and conclusions.

In total, our dataset consisted of 8736 reference sentences and 175801 variants. We estimated lexical surprisal using trigram models trained on 1 million Hindi sentences from EMILLE Corpus (Baker et al., 2002) using the SRILM toolkit (Stolcke, 2002). Good-Turing discounting was used for smoothing. Syntactic surprisal was estimated using an incremental dependency parser (Agrawal et al., 2017) having state-of-the-art unlabelled dependency parsing accuracy. As discussed in the cited work, the per-word syntactic surprisal estimates were also significant predictors of various measures of reading time.

5 Experiments

In this section, we describe our experiments quantifying the impact of the UID measures (proposed in Section 3) on word order choice.

5.1 Pairwise Classification using Logistic Regression

In order to investigate the individual and collective impact of our UID predictors and controls (lexical and syntactic surprisal), we trained and tested logistic regression models for the binary classification task of choosing corpus sentences vs. non-corpus variants. Since our data set is hugely unbalanced, with many more non-corpus than corpus variants, we use a technique from (Joachims, 2002) to effectively convert it into a balanced setting. We created equal numbers of ordered pairs of the types *<corpus, non-corpus>* and *<non-corpus, corpus>* (both sentences in each pair being variants of each other). Feature values of the first sentence in each ordered pair were subtracted from the second sentence in that pair. For a more detailed illustration, please refer to (Rajkumar et al., 2016). This technique also enables feature values of sentences of differing lengths to be centered. The binary classification task is then to identify

	UIDglob	UIDloc	UIDglobNorm	UIDlocNorm	UIDlocPrevNorm
Lexical surprisal	-0.64	-0.58	0.61	0.35	0.02
Syntactic surprisal	-0.46	-0.40	0.19	0.13	0.01

Table 2: Pearson correlation coefficient between: 1. Lexical surprisal and lexical UID measures (Row 1) 2. Syntactic surprisal and syntactic UID measures (Row 2)

each given pair's type, i.e., given such a pair, identify whether the corpus sentence is the first one or the second one. So this can be seen as a way of training a logistic regression model to do pairwise ranking of sentences. The transformed version of the dataset consisted of 175801 data points. Subsequently, we used the python *scikit-learn* toolkit (v0.16.1) to train logistic regression models on this dataset in order to predict the corpus choice sentence. We performed 27-fold cross-validation for classification, wherein the dataset was divided into 27 distinct parts and each part was tested using models trained on the other 26 sections (100 training iterations using *lbfgs* solver).

Table 1 shows the classification results for models trained on different subsets of our features, including both the lexical and syntactic versions of each feature (at both word and constituent levels). Now, we describe the performance of the word-based lexical and syntactic UID measures (middle column of Table 1). The individual classification results show that the best performing feature is lexical surprisal, which predicts the reference sentence in 89.96% of the cases. The negative sign associated with the regression coefficients of both lexical and syntactic surprisal shows that reference sentences are associated with lower surprisal (lower processing difficulty) compared to the variants. For the UID hypothesis to hold true, the regression coefficients of our UID measures should be associated with a positive sign, signifying greater increase in uniformity of information across the sentence. Now we turn to a discussion of the performance of our UID measures, individually as well as in conjunction with lexical surprisal.

Amongst the lexical UID measures, the normalized global UID measure (UIDglobNorm) is the top performing feature (73.04% classification accuracy), while the raw version (UIDglob) comes very close (72.19% accuracy). The accuracy and direction of the UID measures can be attributed to the correlation of these UID measures with surprisal. Table 2 depicts the Pearson's coefficient of correlation between UID measures at the sentence-level and the corresponding surprisal values. For both lexical and syntactic UID measures, normalization results in the direction of the correlation with surprisal being reversed. Both UIDglob and UIDglobNorm measures are moderately correlated with lexical surprisal and hence their performance is much above random chance. UIDglob has a positive regression coefficient, which shows that reference sentences display tendency to maximize uniformity in the spread of information (i.e. minimize negative variance) compared to variant sentences. This is consistent with the UID hypothesis. UIDglob is negatively correlated with lexical surprisal and hence the direction of the effect is also opposite to that of lexical surprisal, which has a negative coefficient as stated above. However, UIDglobNorm has a negative regression coefficient and this goes counter to the UID hypothesis. Thus, normalization has resulted in a measure which exhibits positive correlation with lexical surprisal, resulting in a tendency to mirror lexical surprisal for the task of discriminating between corpus and non-corpus variants. The raw local UID measure (UIDloc) comes very close with 71.22% performance. Both its normalized counterparts (UIDlocNorm and UIDlocPrevNorm) result in considerably lower performance compared to the raw local measure. This difference can again be explained by normalization resulting in UIDlocNorm having low correlation with lexical surprisal and UIDlocPrevNorm being uncorrelated with lexical surprisal. In fact, previous word-based local normalization (UIDlocPrevNorm) resulted in accuracy close to random chance.

The classification performance of syntactic surprisal is very low (56.48%) compared to that of lexical surprisal. We attribute this is to the fact that our syntactic surprisal estimates are derived from an incremental dependency parser (Agrawal et al., 2017), while the task involves constituent ordering. Consequently, all the syntactic UID measures also result in classification accuracy close to 50%. The direction of the individual syntactic UID measures also mirror the direction of correlation between these UID measures and syntactic surprisal (as in the case of the lexical UID measures).

Now, we turn to interpreting the impact of UID measures in combination with lexical surprisal. In order to discern the impact of UID measures over and above lexical surprisal (a strong predictor of Hindi syntactic choice), we added each UID measure into a classification model containing only lexical surprisal. The results are shown in the bottom row of Table 1. The differences in classification performance between each UID measure and lexical surprisal is not statistically significant. It is evident from the classification results that all the UID measures (both syntactic and lexical) are not adding anything useful beyond overall lexical surprisal estimated using trigrams. Our results involving global UID measures are in line with similar findings obtained by other researchers for a variety of languages. Gildea and Jaeger (2015) document that for American English (written and spoken), German, Arabic (Modern Standard), Czech and Mandarin Chinese, there is no evidence that the variance of Shannon information across words within sentences is lower than expected by chance.

Another puzzle which emerged out of our experimental results is that the effect of many our UID measures is not in the expected direction. The negative regression coefficients associated with all the lexical UID measures (and two of our syntactic UID measures) in conjunction with lexical surprisal show that the reference sentences actually display a lack of uniformity of information, going counter to the UID hypothesis. In the following section, we present evidence that these quirky effects are linked with structures involving non-canonical word order patterns in Hindi.

5.2 UID and Non-canonical Word Order Patterns

Construction (#data points)	Predictor(s)	Weight(s)	%Accuracy
DO fronting (1741)	Lexical surprisal	-0.52	79.15
	+UIDloc (*lex*)	-0.66, -0.35	80.07
	+UIDloc (*syn*)	-0.67, -0.45	81.05
IO fronting (1460)	Lexical surprisal	-0.14	86.57
	+UIDlocNorm (*lex*)	-0.89, -1.97	87.34
	+UIDlocNorm (*syn*)	-0.88, -1.50	87.05

Table 3: UID and non-canonical word order choices ('+' stands for 'Lexical surprisal +')

Free word order languages are also characterized by non-canonical word order patterns. Hindi largely follows the Subject, Indirect Object (IO), Direct Object (DO) and Verb order (Mohanan and Mohanan, 1994). But both direct and indirect object fronting (involving movement of objects to precede subjects), occur rarely, resulting in marked structures. Vasishth (2004) shows how increased reading times at the verb are attested for Hindi object-fronted structures (compared to the base word order), both with and without context. In the light of this finding, we examine the impact of our word-based UID measures on sentence pairs where the reference sentence has the following non-canonical orders and the variant has the corresponding canonical order: 1. Direct object (DO) fronting 2. Indirect object (IO) fronting.

Table 3 presents our classification results for each construction above for models trained and tested only on data points belonging to those constructions. This was motivated by the plan to examine the properties of these constructions in question. We provide the percentage accuracy and direction of the best-performing UID measure relative to lexical surprisal. In the case of direct object fronting, the UIDloc measures (both lexical and syntactic) outperform all the other UID measures. For indirect object fronting, the normalized local UID measures (both lexical and syntactic) help induce improvements in classification accuracy over lexical surprisal. All the aforementioned accuracy gains over lexical surprisal are statistically significant as per McNemar's χ-square test (two-tailed $p < 0.001$). As evinced from Table 3, in all these cases, the direction of the UID effects are not in the expected direction, *i.e.*, reference sentences (involving non-canonical DO/IO-subject-verb orders) display spikes and troughs in their lexical and syntactic surprisal values.

This result connects directly to prior work (Maurits et al., 2010), which makes a prediction that languages with object-first orders are non-optimal in ensuring an even spread of information across the entire sentence. They define a toy language consisting of only permutations of three words (viz., subject, object and verb). Then they create data for this toy language using English and Japanese child-directed speech obtained from the CHILDES corpus. Subsequently, they demonstrate that in object-first orders, the first word (*i.e.*, the object) is associated with a disproportionate quantum of information because objects tend to predict ensuing subjects and verbs very accurately. Subsequent words (especially the final verb) are thus rendered to be very uninformative, resulting in a significant trough after the object. For example, the object *water*, restricts predictions related to verbs to a few possibilities like *drink*. In contrast, encountering a verb like *drink* first can trigger multiple object candidates like *water*, *juice* or *tea*. Our own written Hindi data is very different from the toy language created out of the child-directed speech data. Yet, the aforementioned pattern of spikes/troughs prior to the verb is attested in our data as exemplified in the reference-variant pair of sentences below:

(1)   a.   POTA kanoon-ko pichle   raajag sarakaar-ne   aatankavaad-se nipatane va aatankee gatividhiyon-par
             POTA law-ACC previous central government-ERG terrorism-OBL tackle   and terrorist activities-LOC
             lagaam-ke liye laagoo kiya tha.
             restrain-PSP   imposed

             The POTA law had been implemented by the previous central government for tackling terrorism and restraining terrorist activities.

      b.   pichle raajag sarakaar-ne POTA kanoon-ko aatankavaad-se nipatane va aatankee gatividhiyon-par lagaam-ke liye laagoo kiya tha

Here, the reference sentence with object fronting (Example 1a above) has slightly higher lexical surprisal (*i.e.*, higher processing cost) of 41.92 bits compared to the variant (Example 1b with canonical ordering) having lexical surprisal of 41.55 bits. In this case, adding the local UID features (syntactic and lexical) to a model containing lexical surprisal, helps the combined model offset this disadvantage of higher surprisal associated with the reference sentence (in comparison to the variant) and select it. Figure 1 in the Appendix shows the lexical information density changes across the referent-variant pair shown above. In the above examples, in the reference sentence, the first word *POTA* (acronym for Prevention of Terrorism Act) has a higher information density value of 4.5 bits compared to the first word *pichle* (adjective meaning *previous*) in the variant (3.7 bits). However, the acronym is predictive of the word *kanoon* (law), which thus has a low information density value of 1.6 bits, resulting in a trough in the reference sentence. Further research needs to be conducted in order to investigate the information theoretic properties of words belonging to different semantic classes. The above examples also reveal a major lacuna in our current surprisal measures. They do not factor in extra-sentential information going beyond the local lexical and syntactic context. Thus, a word might have a very low probability (higher surprisal) in a particular two-word or local syntactic context, but it might have been mentioned previously in one of the preceding sentences in the discourse context. In Example 1a, the first word (acronym *POTA*) has a high information density value (*i.e.* low trigram probability), but is actually mentioned two sentences before in the preceding context. More generally, out of 13,274 sentences in the entire HUTB, 71.20% sentences contain atleast one content word which is mentioned in the preceding sentence. Persistence effects in language production are a well studied phenomenon (Szmrecsanyi, 2005) and in future we intend to deploy richer models of surprisal estimates incorporating discourse context. One would also expect factors such as the syntactic form of a sentence, its length, focus, or the topic addressed to play a major role in the distribution of information density. These can also be integrated into our models.

5.3   Choice Points in Language Production: Constituent Boundaries

In our UID measures (defined in Section 3) we have made the crucial assumption that individual words are the 'grain size' over which a speaker will spread the information to be transmitted uniformly. While word-based incrementality is taken as standard for language comprehension, language production might exhibit constituent-level incrementality as suggested by psycholinguistic evidence presented by (Hildebrandt et al., 1999). Given that we might often pause at chunk boundaries, this may be effectively allowing for a lowering of information density *in time*. Also, it could be the case that producers are using these spikes to demarcate constituent boundaries.

In order to investigate the above hypothesis, we performed classification experiments using UID measures (both lexical and syntactic) based on constituent boundaries in order to distinguish between corpus and non-corpus sentences. We computed values of constituent-based UID features by plugging in values of information density of the first words of each constituent into the formulae described in Section 2. These new UID features also do not result in significant gains in classification accuracy over and above lexical surprisal as shown in Table 1 (far right column). The individual performance of constituent-based UID measures are also much worse than the corresponding figures involving the all-words UID measures. The direction of the lexical UID features also suggest the anti-UID effect evinced in the case of the word-based UID measures discussed previously. All these results suggests that UID (as quantified by us) does not shape word order choices in Hindi. We now turn to a discussion of possible theoretical reasons for this.

6 Discussion

In recent years, the UID hypothesis has gained lot of attention as a cognitively plausible account of syntactic reduction phenomena (Levy and Jaeger, 2007; Jaeger, 2010) as well as an explanation for the distribution of various types of word order patterns in language (Maurits et al., 2010). However, our results call into question the role of UID as a predictor of word order choices in Hindi. In this section, we elaborate on various reasons for this.

Ferrer-i-Cancho (2017) establishes that the UID hypothesis is a particular case of the Constant Entropy Rate (CER) hypothesis stated in Genzel and Charniak (2002) and provides a mathematical critique of CER (and hence UID) as applied to word order. The crux of Ferrer-i-Cancho's argument is that for predicting the next element in a sequence, CER and UID are applicable for periodic sequences (the best case in terms of predictability, where a block is repeated as in *abcabcabc...*) as well as sequences of independent identically distributed (*i.i.d.*) elements (the worst case). *i.i.d.* sequences can be random sequences (like scrambled texts) or perfectly homogeneous sequences (example *aaaa...*). Thus, Ferrer-i-Cancho (2017) refutes both CER and derivate UID hypotheses as principles explaining word order on the grounds that these hold for sequences that do not have any kind of order. As a consequence, CER (and UID) cannot be defining characteristics of real texts. Ferrer-i-Cancho (2017) also explains how a modern theory of language and word order in particular consist of a collection of well-established principles and their interactions. Notably, different word order principles are often in conflict with one another. Thus, anti-UID effects are only to be expected. Ferrer-i-Cancho et al. (2013) discuss how probabilities and conditional entropies of natural language might potentially be competing principles with one favouring UID while the other is working against it. Recently, we performed similar experiments on English using syntactic choice data from WSJ and Brown corpora used in Rajkumar et al. (2016). In English also, preliminary results indicate that our UID measures do not significantly improve upon the performance of lexical and syntactic surprisal. This leads further credence to the critique of UID presented above.

Ferrer-i-Cancho (2017) further discusses the empirical success of UID in accounting for syntactic reduction phenomena by showing that reduction is a special case of the principle of compression of codes in standard information theory. Higher order compression allows for codes of length 0, viz. full reduction as in the case of *that*-omission in complement clauses (Jaeger, 2010). First order compressions involve codes of length greater than zero as in the case of contractions like *he's* (instead of the full form *he is*) explained using UID in Frank and Jaeger (2008). Thus, our own empirical results and the recent critique of UID in the literature suggest that while UID might be effective in explaining syntactic reduction phenomena in natural language, its contribution towards a theory of word order is doubtful.

7 Conclusions and Future work[2]

Our results suggest that the UID hypothesis for word order (as quantified by our UID measures) does not shape word order choices in Hindi. Our experiments reveal that these UID measures do not contribute over and above lexical surprisal, a control factor, for predicting the corpus sentence. Moreover, anti-UID effects are attested in the case of object fronting, constructions known to be not favourable to distributing the information uniformly across the utterance. In order to model word order, in the near future we plan to test the efficacy of discourse-context enhanced surprisal estimated using more advanced models like RNNs and LSTMs. We also intend to explore other measures of variation like the *coefficient of variation*, and test our hypotheses on typologically diverse languages from South Asia.

---

[2]We are grateful to Florian Jaeger and the anonymous reviewers of this workshop and CMCL-2018 for their feedback. The fourth author acknowledges support from IISER Bhopal's Faculty Initiation Grant (IISERB/R&D/2018-19/77).

References

Rama Kant Agnihotri. 2007. *Hindi: An Essential Grammar*. Essential Grammars. Routledge.

Arpit Agrawal, Sumeet Agarwal, and Samar Husain. 2017. Role of expectation and working memory constraints in hindi comprehension: An eyetracking corpus analysis. *Journal of Eye Movement Research*, 10(2).

Paul Baker, Andrew Hardie, Tony McEnery, Hamish Cunningham, and Robert Gaizauskas, 2002. *EMILLE: a 67-million word corpus of Indic languages: data collection, mark-up and harmonization.*, pages 819–827. Lancaster University.

Rajesh Bhatt, Bhuvana Narasimhan, Martha Palmer, Owen Rambow, Dipti Misra Sharma, and Fei Xia. 2009. A multi-representational and multi-layered treebank for hindi/urdu. In *Proceedings of the Third Linguistic Annotation Workshop*, ACL-IJCNLP '09, pages 186–189, Stroudsburg, PA, USA. Association for Computational Linguistics.

Marisa Ferrara Boston, John T. Hale, Shravan Vasishth, and Reinhold Kliegl. 2011. Parallel processing and sentence comprehension difficulty. *Language and Cognitive Processes*, 26(3):301–349.

Michael Xavier Collins. 2014. Information density and dependency length as complementary cognitive models. *Journal of Psycholinguistic Research*, 43(5):651–681, Oct.

August Fenk and Gertraud Fenk-Oczlon. 1980. Konstanz im kurzzeitgedchtnis - konstanz im sprachlichen informationsflu? *Zeitschrift fr experimentelle und angewandte Psychologie*, 27:400–414, 01.

Gertraud Fenk-Oczlon. 2001. Familiarity, information flow, and linguistic form. In J.L. Bybee and P.J. Hopper, editors, *Frequency and the Emergence of Linguistic Structure*, volume 45, pages 431–448. John Benjamins Publishing Company, 01.

Ramon Ferrer-i-Cancho, ukasz Dbowski, and Fermn Moscoso del Prado Martn. 2013. Constant conditional entropy and related hypotheses. *Journal of Statistical Mechanics: Theory and Experiment*, 2013(07):L07001.

Ramon Ferrer-i-Cancho. 2017. The placement of the head that maximizes predictability. an information theoretic approach. *Glottometrics*, 39:38–71, 05.

A. Frank and T.F. Jaeger. 2008. Speaking rationally: Uniform information density as an optimal strategy for language production. *Cogsci. Washington, DC: CogSci.*

Dmitriy Genzel and Eugene Charniak. 2002. Entropy rate constancy in text. In *Proceedings of the 40th Annual Meeting on Association for Computational Linguistics*, ACL '02, pages 199–206, Stroudsburg, PA, USA. Association for Computational Linguistics.

Daniel Gildea and T. Florian Jaeger. 2015. Human languages order information efficiently. *CoRR*, abs/1510.02823.

John Hale. 2001. A probabilistic Earley parser as a psycholinguistic model. In *Proceedings of the second meeting of the North American Chapter of the Association for Computational Linguistics on Language technologies*, NAACL '01, pages 1–8, Pittsburgh, Pennsylvania. Association for Computational Linguistics.

Bernd Hildebrandt, Hans-Jürgen Eikmeyer, Gert Rickheit, and Petra Weiß. 1999. Inkrementelle sprachrezeption. In Ipke Wachsmuth and Bernhard Jung, editors, *KogWis99: Proceedings der 4. Fachtagung der Gesellschaft für Kognitionswissenschaft*, pages 19–24. Bielefeld University.

T. Florian Jaeger and Esteban Buz. in press. Signal reduction and linguistic encoding. In Eva M. Fernandez and Helen Smith Cairns, editors, *Handbook of Psycholinguistics*, page To appear. Wiley-Blackwell.

T. Florian Jaeger. 2010. Redundancy and reduction: Speakers manage information density. *Cognitive Psychology*, 61(1):23–62, August.

Thorsten Joachims. 2002. Optimizing search engines using clickthrough data. In *Proceedings of the Eighth ACM SIGKDD International Conference on Knowledge Discovery and Data Mining*, KDD '02, pages 133–142, New York, NY, USA. ACM.

Y. Kachru. 2006. *Hindi*. London Oriental and African language library. John Benjamins Publishing Company.

Roger Levy and T. Florian Jaeger. 2007. Speakers optimize information density through syntactic reduction. In B. Schölkopf, J. Platt, and T. Hoffman, editors, *Advances in Neural Information Processing Systems 19*. MIT Press, Cambridge, MA.

Roger Levy. 2008. Expectation-based syntactic comprehension. *Cognition*, 106(3):1126 – 1177.

Luke Maurits, Dan Navarro, and Amy Perfors. 2010. Why are some word orders more common than others? a uniform information density account. In J. Lafferty, C. K. I. Williams, J. Shawe-Taylor, R.S. Zemel, and A. Culotta, editors, *Advances in Neural Information Processing Systems 23*, pages 1585–1593.

K.P. Mohanan and Tara Mohanan. 1994. Issues in word order in south asian languages: Enriched phrase structure or multidimensionality? In Miriam Butt, Tracy Holloway King, and Gillian Ramchand, editors, *Theoretical perspectives on word order in South Asian languages*, pages 153–184. Center for the Study of Language and Information, Stanford, CA.

Günter Neumann and Gertjan van Noord. 1992. Self-monitoring with reversible grammars. In *Proceedings of the 14th conference on Computational linguistics - Volume 2*, COLING '92, pages 700–706, Nantes, France. Association for Computational Linguistics.

Joakim Nivre. 2008. Algorithms for deterministic incremental dependency parsing. *Comput. Linguist.*, 34(4):513–553, December.

Rajakrishnan Rajkumar, Marten van Schijndel, Michael White, and William Schuler. 2016. Investigating locality effects and surprisal in written english syntactic choice phenomena. *Cognition*, 155:204–232.

C. E. Shannon. 1948. A mathematical theory of communication. *Bell system technical journal*, 27.

Andreas Stolcke. 2002. SRILM — An extensible language modeling toolkit. In *Proc. ICSLP-02*.

Benedikt Szmrecsanyi. 2005. Language users as creatures of habit: A corpus-based analysis of persistence in spoken english. *Corpus Linguistics and Linguistic Theory*, 1:113–150.

S. Vasishth. 2004. Discourse context and word order preferences in Hindi. *Yearbook of South Asian Languages*, pages 113–127.

A   Appendix

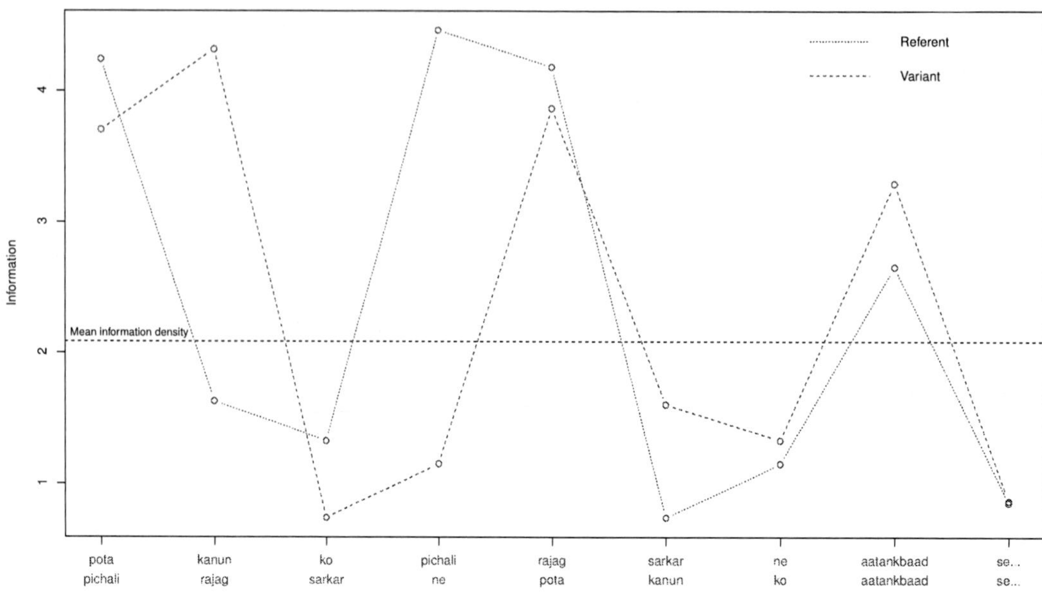

Figure 1: Information variation in bits/word across a pair of reference-variant sentences

Investigating the importance of linguistic complexity features across different datasets related to language learning

Ildikó Pilán
Språkbanken, University of Gothenburg
Sweden
ildiko.pilan@gu.se

Elena Volodina
Språkbanken, University of Gothenburg
Sweden
elena.volodina@gu.se

Abstract

We present the results of our investigations aiming at identifying the most informative linguistic complexity features for classifying language learning levels in three different datasets. The datasets vary across two dimensions: the size of the instances (texts vs. sentences) and the language learning skill they involve (reading comprehension texts vs. texts written by learners themselves). We present a subset of the most predictive features for each dataset, taking into consideration significant differences in their per-class mean values and show that these subsets lead not only to simpler models, but also to an improved classification performance. Furthermore, we pinpoint fourteen central features that are good predictors regardless of the size of the linguistic unit analyzed or the skills involved, which include both morpho-syntactic and lexical dimensions.

1 Introduction

Linguistic complexity, especially in cross-linguistic studies, is often approached in absolute terms, describing complexity as a property of a linguistic system in terms of e.g. number of contrastive sounds. In this paper, however, we investigate a *relative* type of linguistic complexity from a cognitive perspective, our focus being the ability of L2 learners to process or produce certain linguistic elements in writing at different stages of proficiency. We operationalize the term *linguistic complexity* as the set of lexico-semantic, morphological and syntactic characteristics reflected in texts (or sentences) that determine the magnitude of the language skills and competences required to process or produce them. In this work, we use linguistic complexity analysis as a means to predict second language learning (L2) levels. The scale of learning (*proficiency*) levels adopted here is the CEFR, the Common European Framework of Reference for Languages (Council of Europe, 2001) which proposes a six-point scale of proficiency levels: from A1 (beginner) to C2 (advanced) level.

Large corpora in the language learning domain are rather scarce due to either copy-right issues, privacy reasons or the need for digitizing them. For the Swedish language, a number of resources have become available recently (Volodina et al., 2014; Volodina et al., 2016b), which, although somewhat small in size, encompass texts involving different skills and CEFR levels. This allows for investigations about the similarities and differences between linguistic complexity observable at different proficiency levels for different skill types, namely *receptive* skills, required when learners process passages produced by others and *productive* skills, when learners produce the texts themselves. We perform linguistic complexity analyses across two different dimensions: the type of learner skills involved when dealing with the texts and the size of the linguistic context investigated. In the latter case, we carry out experiments both at the text and at the sentence level.

Throughout the years, a large number of linguistic features related to complexity has been proposed. Typically, out of the features suggested for a specific task some are more useful than others. Eliminating redundant features can result in simpler and improved models that are not only faster, but might also generalize better on unseen data (Witten et al., 2011, 308). Such selection can also contribute to understand further the main factors playing role in linguistic complexity, which can be a useful means for

Proceedings of the Workshop on Linguistic Complexity and Natural Language Processing, pages 49–58
Santa Fe, New Mexico, USA, August 25, 2018.

determining whether non-native speakers can understand or produce certain linguistic input at different learning levels. In this paper, we investigate therefore the importance of individual linguistic complexity features for predicting proficiency levels across different L2 datasets. The two main research questions we investigate are: (i) Which linguistic complexity features are most useful for determining proficiency levels for each L2 dataset? (ii) Are there features that are relevant regardless of the context size and the type of skill considered? Our contributions include, on the one hand, a subset of the most informative features for each dataset whose use leads to improved classification results. On the other hand, we identify some lexical, morphological and syntactic features that are good indicators of complexity across all three datasets, namely, reading comprehension texts, essays and sentences.

In Section 2, we provide an overview of previous work related to linguistic complexity analysis, followed by the description of our datasets in Section 3. In Section 4, we present the set of features used and highlight their relevance for modeling linguistic complexity in the L2 context. We then describe our experiments and their results in Section 5, presenting the most informative features and their effect on classification performance. Finally, we conclude our results and outline future work in Section 6.

2 Previous literature on linguistic complexity for predicting L2 levels

Expert-written (receptive) texts In the L2 context, specific scales reflecting progress in language proficiency have been proposed. One such scale is the CEFR, introduced in section 1. An alternative to the CEFR is the 7-point scale of the Interagency Language Roundtable (ILR), common in the United States. In Table 1, we provide an overview of studies targeting L2 receptive complexity and compare the target language, the type and amount of training data and the methods used. The studies are ordered alphabetically based on the target language of the linguistic complexity analysis. We only include previous work here that shares the following characteristics: (i) texts rather than single sentences are the unit of analysis; (ii) receptive linguistic complexity is measured; and (iii) NLP tools are combined with machine learning algorithms. Under dataset size, we report the number of texts used (except for Heilman et al. (2007)), where whole books were employed), followed by the number of tokens in parenthesis when available.

Study	Target language	CEFR	Dataset size in # texts	Text type	# levels	Method
Salesky and Shen (2014)	Arabic, Dari English, Pashto	No	4 × 1400	Non-L2	7	Regr.
Sung et al. (2015)	Chinese	Yes	1578	L2	6	Classif.
Heilman et al. (2007)	English	No	4 books (200,000)	L2	4	Regr.
Huang et al. (2011)	English	No	187	Both	6	Regr.
Xia et al. (2016)	English	Yes	331	L2	5 (A2-C2)	Both
Zhang et al. (2013)	English	No	15	Non-L2	1-10	Regr.
François and Fairon (2012)	French	Yes	1852 (510,543)	L2	6	Classif.
Branco et al. (2014)	Portuguese	Yes	110 (12,673)	L2	5 (A1-C1)	Regr.
Curto et al. (2015)	Portuguese	Yes	237 (25,888)	L2	5 (A1-C1)	Classif.
Karpov et al. (2014)	Russian	Yes	219	Both	4 (A1-B1, C2)	Classif.
Reynolds (2016)	Russian	Yes	4689	Both	6	Classif.
Pilán et al. (2016)	Swedish	Yes	867	L2	5 (A1-C1)	Both

Table 1: An overview of studies on L2 receptive complexity.

CEFR-based studies have been more commonly treated as a classification problem, a popular choice of classifier being support vector machines (SVM). A particular aspect distinguishing Xia et al. (2016) from the rest of the studies mentioned in Table 1 is the idea of using L1 data to improve the classification of L2 texts. For the sake of comparability, the information in Table 1 describes only the experiments using the L2 data reported in this study. The state-of-the-art performance reported for the CEFR-based classification described in the studies included in Table 1 ranges between 75% and 80% accuracy (Curto et al., 2015; Sung et al., 2015; Xia et al., 2016; Pilán et al., 2016a).

A large number of features have been proposed and tested in this context. Count-based measures (e.g. sentence and token length, type-token ratio) and syntactic features (e.g. dependency length) have been confirmed to be influencing factors in L2 complexity (Curto et al., 2015; Reynolds, 2016). Lexical information based on either n-gram models (Heilman et al., 2007) or frequency information from word lists (François and Fairon, 2012; Reynolds, 2016; Salesky and Shen, 2014) and Google search results (Huang et al., 2011) has proven to be, however, one of the most predictive dimensions. Heilman et al. (2007) found that lexical features outperform grammatical ones, which, although more important for L2 than L1 complexity, still remain less predictive for L2 English complexity. Nevertheless, the authors mention that this may depend on the morphological richness of a language. Reynolds (2016), in fact, finds that morphological features are among the most influential ones for L2 Russian texts.

Learner-written (productive) texts Similarly to L2 texts targeting reading skills, also texts produced by L2 learners manifest varying degrees of complexity at different stages of proficiency. Typically however, receptive linguistic complexity is somewhat higher than its productive counterpart for a learner at a given CEFR level (Barrot, 2015). Previous studies aiming at classifying CEFR levels in learner-written texts include Hancke and Meurers (2013) for L2 German and Vajjala and Lõo (2014) for L2 Estonian. The most predictive features for L2 German include lexical and morphological features. Morphological features (e.g. amount of distinct cases used) are also among the most informative ones for L2 Estonian at all L2 development stages. A fundamental difference between assessing receptive and productive texts is that, while receptive texts are expected to be relatively error free, the latter ones typically contain a varying amount of L2 errors, which have also been used to inform features. Errors are usually counted based on the output of a spell checker (Hancke and Meurers, 2013; Tack et al., 2017) or by using hand-crafted rules (Tack et al., 2017).

Smaller linguistic units Besides the text-level analyses in Table 1, studies targeting smaller units also appear in the literature. Linguistic complexity in single sentences from an L2 perspective has been explored in Karpov et al. (2014) and in Pilán et al. (2016a). Both studies are CEFR-related, but rather than classifying sentences into individual CEFR levels, a binary distinction is made (below or at B1 level vs. above B1). In Pilán et al. (2016a), we report 63% accuracy for a 5-way CEFR level classification of Swedish coursebook sentences. As for productive complexity, research on the automatic assessment of short answers to open-ended questions in terms of using CEFR has been investigated in Tack et al. (2017) for L2 English. The authors proposed an ensemble method consisting of integrating the votes of a number of traditional classification methods into a single prediction. Sentence and word length, lexical features and information about the age of acquisition of words were found especially predictive.

3 Datasets

3.1 Text-level datasets

We used two L2 Swedish corpora consisting of texts in our experiments: SweLL (Volodina et al., 2016b) comprised of essays written by L2 learners and COCTAILL (Volodina et al., 2014) containing L2 course-books authored or adapted by experts for L2 learners. The SweLL corpus consists of essays produced by adult learners of L2 Swedish on a variety of topics (TEXT-E). From the coursebook corpus, we only include whole texts meant for reading comprehension practice (TEXT-R) since the linguistic annotation of other coursebook elements (e.g. gap-filling exercises) may be prone to automatic linguistic annotation errors. These two corpora cover five CEFR levels (A1 to C1). Each SweLL essay has been assigned a CEFR level by teachers. For reading texts, CEFR levels were derived from the level of the lesson (chapter) they occur in. It is worth mentioning that these two corpora are *independent* from each other, i.e. the essays written by the learners are not based on, or inspired by, the reading passages. The distribution of texts per type and CEFR level in the datasets is shown in Table 2. The total number of tokens in the coursebook-based dataset was 289,312, while in the learner essay data it was 43,033.

3.2 A teacher-evaluated dataset of sentences

At the sentence level, we use a small dataset[1] (SENT) based on the user evaluation of a corpus example selection system, HitEx, which we described in detail in Pilán et al. (2016b). HitEx aims at identifying

---

[1]The dataset is available at https://github.com/IldikoPilan/sent_cefr.

sentences from corpora suitable as exercise items. The sentences in this dataset have been automatically assessed for their CEFR level and have been filtered for their well-formedness, independence from the rest of their textual context and some additional lexical and structural criteria (e.g. abbreviations, interrogative form) using HitEx. Out of the original 330 sentences from the evaluation material, we only included in this dataset the subset of sentences: (i) that were found overall suitable (with an evaluation score $>=$ 2.5 out of 4); and (ii) where a majority of teachers agreed with the CEFR level assigned automatically by HitEx. This subset was complemented with 90 sentences for the otherwise insufficiently represented A1 level from the COCTAILL corpus. Only individually occurring sentences in lists and non-gapped exercises were considered, thus these are not a subset of the text-level dataset described above. The distribution of sentences per CEFR level in the dataset is presented in Table 2. The total number of tokens in the dataset is 4,060.

Writer	Unit	A1	A2	B1	B2	C1	Total
Learner	**Texts**	16	83	75	74	88	**336**
Expert	**Texts**	49	157	258	288	115	**867**
Expert	**Sentences**	98	82	58	92	45	**375**

Table 2: CEFR-level annotated Swedish datasets.

All three corpora are equipped also with automatic linguistic annotation which includes lemmatization, part-of-speech (POS) tagging and dependency parsing based on the $Sparv^2$ pipeline.

4 A flexible feature set for linguistic complexity analysis

In this section, we provide a detailed description of the set of features used and relate them to cognitive aspects of linguistic complexity. The feature set is "flexible" in the sense that it can be applied to different types of L2 data and units of analysis (e.g. texts or sentences) since it does not incorporate text-level features (e.g. discourse-related aspects) or learner language specific ones (e.g. L2 error features). The feature set is comprised of 61 features in total, which we have previously used for CEFR classification experiments also in Pilán et al. (2016c). Table 3 shows the complete feature set divided into five sub-categories based on the type of NLP tools and resources used: *count-based*, *lexical*, *morphological*, *syntactic* and *semantic*.

4.1 Count-based features

The feature set includes seven indicators that are based on simple counts or traditional readability measures. One such measure for Swedish is *LIX* (*Läsbarhetsindex* 'Readability index') proposed in Björnsson (1968). LIX combines the sum of the average number of words per sentence in the text and the percentage of tokens longer than six characters. Sentence length is measured both as the number of tokens and that of characters. Sentence length can indicate syntactic difficulty and it can be a sign of e.g. multiple clauses or larger noun phrases. Average token (T) length is computed based on the number of characters. Extra-long words, i.e. tokens longer than 13 characters, are also counted since compounding, frequent in Swedish, can result in particularly long words (Heimann Mühlenbock, 2013). Type-token ratio (TTR), the ratio of unique tokens to all tokens, is an indicator of lexical richness (Graesser et al., 2004). A bi-logarithmic and a square root TTR are used which decrease the effect of text and sentence length (Vajjala and Meurers, 2012).

4.2 Word-list based lexical features

Besides richness, the frequency of words also influences lexical complexity as repeated exposure facilitates their processing (Graesser et al., 2004). Frequency information is collected from the KELLY list (Volodina and Kokkinakis, 2012), based on web texts.

---

^{2}`https://spraakbanken.gu.se/sparv/`

COUNT	SYNTACTIC	MORPHOLOGICAL
Sentence length	Avg. DepArc length	Function W INCSC
Avg token length	DepArc Len > 5	Particle INCSC
Extra-long token	Max length DepArc	3SG pronoun INCSC
Nr characters	Right DepArc Ratio	Punctuation INCSC
LIX	Left DepArc Ratio	Subjunction INCSC
Bilog TTR	Modifier variation	PR to N
Square root TTR	Pre-modifier INCSC	PR to PP
LEXICAL	Post-modifier INCSC	Relative structure INCSC
Avg KELLY log freq	Subordinate INCSC	S-V INCSC
A1 lemma INCSC	Relative clause INCSC	S-V to V
A2 lemma INCSC	PP complement INCSC	ADJ INCSC
B1 lemma INCSC	**MORPHOLOGICAL**	ADJ variation
B2 lemma INCSC	Neuter N INCSC	ADV INCSC
C1 lemma INCSC	CJ + SJ INCSC	ADV variation
C2 lemma INCSC	Past PC to V	N INCSC
Difficult W INCSC	Present PC to V	N variation
Difficult N&V INCSC	Past V to V	V INCSC
OOV INCSC	Supine V to V	V variation
No lemma INCSC	Present V to V	Lex T to Nr T
SEMANTIC	Nominal ratio	Lex T to non-lex T
Avg senses per token	N to V	
N senses per N	Modal V to V	

Table 3: Feature set for linguistic complexity assessment in L2 data.

Instead of n-grams, weakly lexicalized features are employed to increase the generalizability of the models on unseen data. Each token is represented by its corresponding CEFR level. Unlike in Pilán et al. (2016c), where we employed KELLY, the per-token CEFR level information is retrieved here from two word lists compiled based on the L2 corpora described in Section 3. To guarantee the independence of the word lists from the datasets, we use SweLLex (Volodina et al., 2016a), a frequency list based on the learner essays when classifying CEFR levels in coursebook texts and SVALex (François et al., 2016), containing frequencies from coursebooks for making predictions on the essays. For sentences, SVALex has been used since it is independent from the dataset, but both reflect receptive linguistic complexity. Frequency distributions in these lists have been mapped to single CEFR levels based on the difference in per-level normalized frequency between adjacent levels as described in Alfter et al. (2016).

Instead of absolute counts, a normalized value, an *incidence score* (INCSC $= \frac{1000}{N_t} \times N_c$) is used to reduce the influence of sentence length, where N_t is the total number of tokens and N_c is the count of a certain category of tokens in the text or sentence (Graesser et al., 2004). The INCSC of *difficult* tokens is also computed, that is, tokens above a certain reference CEFR level, which can be the level of an L2 learner writing a text or whom the text would be presented to as reading material. This value is also computed separately for nouns and verbs, since these are crucial for conveying meaning. Moreover, the INCSC of tokens not present in the L2 word lists, i.e. out-of-vocabulary words (*OOV* INCSC) is also considered as well as the INCSC of non-lemmatized tokens (*No lemma* INCSC).

4.3 Morphological features

Morphological features include not only INCSC of different morpho-syntactic categories, but also variational scores, i.e. the ratio of a category to the ratio of *lexical* tokens: nouns (N), verbs (V), adjectives (ADJ) and adverbs (ADV). Some specific features for L2 Swedish are the ratio of different verb forms to verbs which are typically introduced at varying stages of L2 learning. *S-verbs* (*S-VB*) are a group of Swedish verbs ending in *-s* that are peculiar in terms of morphology and semantics. They indicate either reciprocity, a passive construction or are *deponent* verbs, i.e. verbs active in meaning, but passive in form. Neuter gender nouns are also considered since they can indicate the abstractness of a concept (Graesser et al., 2004). Among relative structures relative adverbs, determiners, pronouns and possessives are counted. *Nominal ratio* (Hultman and Westman, 1977) corresponds to the ratio of nominal categories, i.e. nouns, prepositions (PP) and participles to the ratio of verbal categories, namely pronouns (PR), adverbs, and verbs. Its simplified version is the ratio of nouns to verbs, and it is meant to measure the information load of a text or reveal its genre (e.g. spoken vs. news text). A higher value corresponds to higher degrees of complexity and a more elaborate genre.

INCSC for punctuation marks as well as sub- and conjunctions (SJ, CJ) are also computed since their presence in larger quantities can indicate a more complex syntactic structure. Particles can change the meaning of verbs considerably, similarly to English phrasal verbs (Heimann Mühlenbock, 2013). The INCSC of the third person singular (3SG) pronoun inspired by Zhang et al. (2013) is also included since this is often used referentially, which can further increase the difficulty of processing.

4.4 Syntactic and semantic features

Syntactic aspects are related to readers' working memory load when processing sentences which can be increased by ambiguity or embedded constituents (Graesser et al., 2004). Here, the average length (depth) of dependency arcs (*DepArc*) and their direction is considered. Relative clauses, pre- and post-modifiers (e.g. adjectives and prepositional phrases), prepositional complements as well as subordinates, commonly used in previous research on linguistic complexity (Heimann Mühlenbock, 2013; Schwarm and Ostendorf, 2005), are also counted.

The two semantic features included quantify available word senses per lemma based on the SALDO lexicon (Borin et al., 2013). Both the average number of senses per token and the average number of noun senses per noun are considered. Polysemous words can be demanding for readers as they need to be disambiguated for a full understanding of the sentence (Graesser et al., 2004).

5 Cross-dataset feature selection experiments

In this section, we describe the results of our feature selection experiments on the three datasets presented in Section 3. These experiments differ from the ones we described previously in Pilán et al. (2016a) and Pilán et al. (2016c) in a number of respects. In this work, the worth of individual features is evaluated rather than that of the complete set of features or groups of features. Moreover, as mentioned in section 4, most lexical features are based on L2 word lists rather than KELLY.

5.1 Experimental setup

We use 85% of each dataset for identifying the most informative features (DEV). The reported classification results using this part of the data are based on a stratified 5-fold cross-validation setup, that is, the original distribution of instances per CEFR level in the dataset has been preserved in all folds. We evaluated the generalizability of the selected subset of features on the remaining 15% of the data (TEST). As learning algorithm for these models, we used *LinearSVC* as implemented in scikit-learn (Pedregosa et al., 2011), which has been successfully applied in recent years in a number of NLP areas.

5.2 Feature selection method

As a pre-processing step before training our classifiers, we used a *univariate feature selection* method, also available in scikit-learn, to identify the most informative features scored with *analysis of variance* (ANOVA). This feature selection method is suitable for multi-class problems, it is independent of the learning method used and it has been previously adopted for NLP tasks, e.g. by Carbon et al. (2014). ANOVA is a statistical test that can be used to measure how strong the relationship between each feature and the output class is (CEFR levels in our case). It relies on *F-tests*, which can be employed to score features based on significant differences in their per-class mean values. To detect these differences indicating dependencies, first, the *variance*, i.e. the dispersion of the data in terms of its distance from the mean, is measured both *within* and *between* classes for each feature. Then, the F-statistic can be computed as the ratio of the variance between class means and the variance within a class.

5.3 Results

The results of the models with and without feature selection in terms of accuracy and F_1 are presented in Table 4.

Data	Features	SENT		TEXT-R		TEXT-E	
		Acc	F_1	Acc	F_1	Acc	F_1
DEV	ALL	0.62	0.61	0.68	0.68	0.73	0.71
DEV	K-BEST	0.73	0.71	0.70	0.70	0.81	0.81
TEST	K-BEST	0.81	0.79	0.73	0.73	0.84	0.82
Number of K-BEST		21		54		24	

Table 4: Accuracy with feature selection across datasets.

Reducing the complete set of features to the subset of the most informative ones improved the classification results for all datasets. The most substantial boost (+0.11 accuracy) was obtained for sentences. The models with selected features generalized well also on the held-out test sets. Moreover, while for SENT and TEXT-E only about one third of the features have been selected, almost all features were included in the k number of best ones for TEXT-R. The selected features ranked based on ANOVA are presented in Table 5. For TEXT-R, features with low importance are not listed separately. These are only indicated when they overlap with a feature selected by the other models (with a rank > 24).

Fourteen features were among the most informative ones across all three datasets, which are highlighted in bold in Table 5. One such feature was the count-based measure of square root TTR, thus it seems that a varied way of expression, through e.g. the use of synonyms, is a good indicator of linguistic complexity in the L2 context. Among the word-list based lexical features, besides the proportion of difficult lexica, the amount of tokens at the extremes of the CEFR scale, namely the lowest, A1 level and the advanced, C1 level (the highest available in our L2 lists) were also useful predictors. Interestingly, two out of the three strong indicators of L2 English essay quality identified in Crossley and McNamara (2011) were lexical diversity, closely related to our Square root TTR feature, and lexical frequency, based on the same type of information as our word-list features. Lexical variation in terms of TTR as well as verb variation were also found highly predictive for L2 Estonian learner texts (Vajjala and Lõo, 2014). These findings indicate the predictive strength of these features across languages. Furthermore, syntactic features relative to the length of dependency arcs and verb-related morphological features (e.g. INCSC of participles and s-verbs) were among the k-best for all datasets. Such verb forms are, in fact, typically introduced explicitly to L2 learners at higher CEFR levels (Fasth and Kannermark, 1997). The amount of punctuation and particles was also indicative of complexity. The former can, for example, indicate clause boundaries and hence more complex sentences. Particles, on the other hand, can be challenging for language learners, since they alter the meaning of verbs.

For the two datasets related to receptive skills, SENT and TEXT-R, a number of count features were strongly predictive. Unlike for TEXT-E, sentence length in terms of both the number of tokens and the number of characters were highly informative for determining receptive complexity. Although the proportion of lexical tokens to all tokens was not informative at the sentence level, it proved to be a good indicator of linguistic complexity at the text level. The traditional readability measure, LIX was informative only for TEXT-R, which could be explained by the fact that this dataset was the most similar to the intended use of LIX, namely determining readability at the text level. On the other hand, the other traditional formula, nominal ratio, was more useful across datasets, especially in its simplified version (*N to V*). It would be useful to investigate further whether this also depends on a difference in text genre.

A limitation of our study is the relatively small size of our datasets, which is especially true in the case of the A1 level learner essays. Considering the difficulties in having access to similar types of L2 data, and the extension of our experiments to cross-dataset observations, the results could still provide valuable insights for teaching experts and members of the NLP community targeting similar tasks.

Feature name	Rank		
	SENT	TEXT-R	TEXT-E
Nr characters	1	4	-
Square root TTR	2	7	9
A1 lemma INCSC	3	3	2
Punctuation INCSC	4	11	12
Sentence length	5	5	-
Relative clause	6	> 24	8
Difficult N&V INCSC	7	1	1
Avg. DepArc length	8	10	14
Max length DepArc	9	6	13
Bilog TTR	10	24	-
DepArc Len > 5	11	8	-
S-V INCSC	12	> 24	-
Present PC to V	13	18	17
Past PC to V	14	> 24	18
Particle INCSC	15	> 24	16
V variation	16	15	10
Difficult W INCSC	17	2	4
V INCSC	18	22	-
C1 lemma INCSC	19	> 24	5
3SG pronoun INCSC	20	> 24	-
N to V	21	> 24	20
OOV INCSC	-	9	-
LIX	-	12	-
Extra-long token	-	13	6
Lex T to Nr T	-	14	15
PR to PP	-	16	-
Past V to V	-	17	19
B1 lemma INCSC	-	19	3
Function W INCSC	-	20	-
Right DepArc Ratio	-	21	-
Avg token length	-	23	7
B2 lemma INCSC	-	> 24	11
N senses per N	-	> 24	21
PR to N	-	> 24	22
Nominal ratio	-	> 24	23
N INCSC	-	> 24	24

Table 5: K-best features and their rank across different datasets.

6 Conclusion and future work

In this work, we described the results of a feature selection method applied to different language learning related datasets. We found a small number of features that proved useful across all datasets regardless of the length of the linguistic input or the type of relevant language learning skill. We showed that besides lexical frequency and variation, the length of dependencies and the amount and type of verbs carry valuable information for predicting proficiency levels. To our knowledge, the usefulness of single features across receptive and productive L2 data of different sizes has not been previously explored. We aimed at finding the optimal number and types of features to use in order to boost performance for these types of predictions. An improved CEFR level classification is especially important for its integration into NLP applications aiming at on-the-fly assessment of texts or exercise generation. In the future, extending this investigation of feature importances to datasets in other languages could contribute to a deeper understanding about which indicators are more universally useful. Furthermore, the selected subset of features could be evaluated also with the help of teaching experts to confirm their usefulness.

Acknowledgements

We would like to thank the Royal Swedish Academy of Letters, History and Antiquities for providing a travel grant to the first author via the Wallenberg Foundation.

References

David Alfter, Yuri Bizzoni, Anders Agebjörn, Elena Volodina, and Ildikó Pilán. 2016. From distributions to labels: A lexical proficiency analysis using learner corpora. Number 130 in Proceedings of the joint workshop on NLP for Computer Assisted Language Learning and NLP for Language Acquisition, pages 1–7. Linköping University Electronic Press.

Jessie Saraza Barrot. 2015. Comparing the linguistic complexity in receptive and productive modes. *GEMA Online® Journal of Language Studies*, 15(2).

Carl Hugo Björnsson. 1968. *Läsbarhet*. Liber.

Lars Borin, Markus Forsberg, and Lennart Lönngren. 2013. SALDO: a touch of yin to WordNet's yang. *Language Resources and Evaluation*, 47(4):1191–1211.

António Branco, João Rodrigues, Francisco Costa, João Silva, and Rui Vaz. 2014. Rolling out text categorization for language learning assessment supported by language technology. In *Proceedings of the International Conference on Computational Processing of the Portuguese Language*, pages 256–261. Springer.

Kyle Carbon, Kacyn Fujii, and Prasanth Veerina. 2014. Applications of machine learning to predict Yelp ratings. Stanford Univ., Stanford, CA.

Council of Europe. 2001. *Common European Framework of Reference for Languages: Learning, Teaching, Assessment*. Press Syndicate of the University of Cambridge.

Scott A Crossley and Danielle S McNamara. 2011. Understanding expert ratings of essay quality: Coh-Metrix analyses of first and second language writing. *International Journal of Continuing Engineering Education and Life Long Learning*, 21(2-3):170–191.

Pedro Curto, Nuno J Mamede, and Jorge Baptista. 2015. Automatic text difficulty classifier – Assisting the selection of adequate reading materials for European Portuguese teaching. In *Proceedings of the International Conference on Computer Supported Education*, pages 36–44.

Cecilia Fasth and Anita Kannermark. 1997. *Form i focus: övningsbok i svensk grammatik. Del B*. Folkuniv. Förlag, Lund.

Thomas François and Cédrick Fairon. 2012. An "AI readability" formula for French as a foreign language. In *Proceedings of the 2012 Joint Conference on Empirical Methods in Natural Language Processing and Computational Natural Language Learning*, pages 466–477.

Thomas François, Elena Volodina, Ildikó Pilán, and Anaïs Tack. 2016. SVALex: a CEFR-graded lexical resource for Swedish foreign and second language learners. In *Proceedings of the 10th International Conference on Language Resources and Evaluation*.

Arthur C Graesser, Danielle S McNamara, Max M Louwerse, and Zhiqiang Cai. 2004. Coh-Metrix: Analysis of text on cohesion and language. *Behavior Research Methods*, 36(2):193–202.

Julia Hancke and Detmar Meurers. 2013. Exploring CEFR classification for German based on rich linguistic modeling. In *Learner Corpus Research Conference*, pages 54–56.

Michal J. Heilman, Kevyn Collins-Thompson, Jamie Callan, and Maxine Eskenazi. 2007. Combining lexical and grammatical features to improve readability measures for first and second language texts. In *Proceedings of the North American Chapter of the Association for Computational Linguistics: Human Language Technologies*, pages 460–467.

Katarina Heimann Mühlenbock. 2013. I see what you mean—assessing readability for specific target groups. *Data linguistica*, (24).

Yi-Ting Huang, Hsiao-Pei Chang, Yeali Sun, and Meng Chang Chen. 2011. A robust estimation scheme of reading difficulty for second language learners. In *11th IEEE International Conference on Advanced Learning Technologies (ICALT)*, pages 58–62. IEEE.

Tor G Hultman and Margareta Westman. 1977. *Gymnasistsvenska*. Liber.

Nikolay Karpov, Julia Baranova, and Fedor Vitugin. 2014. Single-sentence readability prediction in Russian. In *International Conference on Analysis of Images, Social Networks and Texts*, pages 91–100. Springer.

Fabian Pedregosa, Gaël Varoquaux, Alexandre Gramfort, Vincent Michel, Bertrand Thirion, Olivier Grisel, Mathieu Blondel, Peter Prettenhofer, Ron Weiss, Vincent Dubourg, et al. 2011. Scikit-learn: Machine learning in Python. *Journal of Machine Learning Research*, 12(Oct):2825–2830.

Ildikó Pilán, Sowmya Vajjala, and Elena Volodina. 2016a. A readable read: automatic assessment of language learning materials based on linguistic complexity. *International Journal of Computational Linguistics and Applications (IJCLA)*, 7(1):143–159.

Ildikó Pilán, Elena Volodina, and Lars Borin. 2016b. Candidate sentence selection for language learning exercises: from a comprehensive framework to an empirical evaluation. *Traitement Automatique des Langues (TAL) Journal, Special issue on NLP for Learning and Teaching*, 57(3):67–91.

Ildikó Pilán, Elena Volodina, and Torsten Zesch. 2016c. Predicting proficiency levels in learner writings by transferring a linguistic complexity model from expert-written coursebooks. In *Proceedings of the 26th International Conference on Computational Linguistics*, pages 2101–2111.

Robert Reynolds. 2016. Insights from Russian second language readability classification: complexity-dependent training requirements, and feature evaluation of multiple categories. In *Proceedings of the 11th Workshop on Innovative Use of NLP for Building Educational Applications*, pages 289–300.

Elizabeth Salesky and Wade Shen. 2014. Exploiting morphological, grammatical, and semantic correlates for improved text difficulty assessment. In *Proceedings of the 9th Workshop on Innovative Use of NLP for Building Educational Applications*, pages 155–162, June.

Sarah E Schwarm and Mari Ostendorf. 2005. Reading level assessment using support vector machines and statistical language models. In *Proceedings of the 43rd Annual Meeting on Association for Computational Linguistics*, pages 523–530.

Yao-Ting Sung, Wei-Chun Lin, Scott Benjamin Dyson, Kuo-En Chang, and Yu-Chia Chen. 2015. Leveling L2 texts through readability: combining multilevel linguistic features with the CEFR. *The Modern Language Journal*, 99(2):371–391.

Anaïs Tack, Thomas François, Sophie Roekhaut, and Cédrick Fairon. 2017. Human and automated CEFR-based grading of short answers. In *Proceedings of the 12th Workshop on Innovative Use of NLP for Building Educational Applications*, pages 169–179.

Sowmya Vajjala and Kaidi Lõo. 2014. Automatic CEFR level prediction for Estonian learner text. *NEALT Proceedings Series Vol. 22*, pages 113–127.

Sowmya Vajjala and Detmar Meurers. 2012. On improving the accuracy of readability classification using insights from second language acquisition. In *Proceedings of the 7th Workshop on Innovative Use of NLP for Building Educational Applications*, pages 163–173.

Elena Volodina and Sofie Johansson Kokkinakis. 2012. Introducing the Swedish Kelly-list, a new lexical e-resource for Swedish. In *Proceedings of the International Conference on Language Resources and Evaluation*, pages 1040–1046.

Elena Volodina, Ildikó Pilán, Stian Rødven Eide, and Hannes Heidarsson. 2014. You get what you annotate: a pedagogically annotated corpus of coursebooks for Swedish as a second language. In *Proceedings of the 3rd workshop on NLP for Computer Assisted Language Learning*, pages 128–144.

Elena Volodina, Ildikó Pilán, Lorena Llozhi, Baptiste Degryse, and Thomas François. 2016a. SweLLex: second language learners' productive vocabulary. In *Proceedings of the joint workshop on NLP for Computer Assisted Language Learning and NLP for Language Acquisition*, number 130, pages 76–84. Linköping University Electronic Press.

Elena Volodina, Ildikó Pilán, Ingegerd Enström, Lorena Llozhi, Peter Lundkvist, Gunlög Sundberg, and Monica Sandell. 2016b. SweLL on the rise: Swedish learner language corpus for European Reference Level studies. In *Proceedings of the Tenth International Conference on Language Resources and Evaluation*.

Ian H Witten, Eibe Frank, Mark A Hall, and Christopher J Pal. 2011. *Data Mining: Practical machine learning tools and techniques*. Morgan Kaufmann.

Menglin Xia, Ekaterina Kochmar, and Ted Briscoe. 2016. Text readability assessment for second language learners. In *Proceedings of the 11th Workshop on Innovative Use of NLP for Building Educational Applications*, pages 12–22.

Lixiao Zhang, Zaiying Liu, and Jun Ni. 2013. Feature-based assessment of text readability. In *7th International Conference on Internet Computing for Engineering and Science (ICICSE)*, pages 51–54. IEEE.

An Approach to Measuring Complexity with a Fuzzy Grammar & Degrees of Grammaticality

Adrià Torrens Urrutia
Universitat Rovira i Virgili, Tarragona, Spain
`adria.torrens@urv.cat`

Abstract

This paper presents an approach to evaluate complexity of a given natural language input by means of a Fuzzy Grammar with some fuzzy logic formulations. Usually, the approaches in linguistics has described a natural language grammar by means of discrete terms. However, a grammar can be explained in terms of degrees by following the concepts of linguistic gradience & fuzziness. Understanding a grammar as a fuzzy or gradient object allows us to establish degrees of grammaticality for every linguistic input. This shall be meaningful for linguistic complexity considering that the less grammatical an input is the more complex its processing will be. In this regard, the degree of complexity of a linguistic input (which is a linguistic representation of a natural language expression) depends on the chosen grammar. The bases of the fuzzy grammar are shown here. Some of these are described by Fuzzy Type Theory. The linguistic inputs are characterized by constraints through a Property Grammar.

1 Introduction: What is Gradience & Fuzziness?

Fuzziness and gradience are pretty similar (if not the same). Gradience has appeared throughout the history of linguistics and can be defined as "a cover term to designate the spectrum of continuous phenomena in language, from categories at the level of the grammar to sounds at the level of phonetics"(Aarts, 2004). Some well-known studies approach gradience to linguistic theory, such as Bolinger (Bolinger, 1961) or Keller (Keller, 2000). However, it is in mathematics where we can find serious formal approaches to describe gradient relations, such as the gradient relation between *tall-short*, *big-small*. Nevertheless, the gradient phenomena in mathematics are called fuzzy phenomena and fuzzy logic is the right tool to formally describe these vague relations, which are also referred to as fuzziness. Zadeh's (Zadeh, 1965) (Zadeh, 1972) mathematical description of gradient phenomena is well-known. He describes the variable semantic values of words, or fuzzy phenomena, in terms of degrees. However, Zadeh did not develop a formal linguistic framework to describe fuzziness in a natural language grammar. A brief methodological description distinguishing both terms is shown:

- A *fuzzy grammar* is a formal framework which defines any kind of linguistic information in any context (as humans do). This framework is set through a flexible constraints' system which describe a natural language grammar. These constraints are known as properties. They work as logical operators that represent grammatical knowledge. They are flexible because they can be violated or satisfied to different degrees.

- *Processing gradience* refers to our capacity to sort out linguistic fuzziness through a scale of degrees. The degree of gradience represents how hard or soft is the violation of a linguistic constraint. In fuzzy logic, this might be referred as truth values, but since we are talking about language, we are going to talk about linguistic gradience as the truth value of an object.

2 Grammaticality as a topic in Complexity

Nowadays the hypothesis of the "equi-complexity" is not as popular as in the 20th century. In fact, several authors such as Mc Worther (Mc Worther, 2001) or Dhal (Dahl, 2004) have challenged this concept.

Proceedings of the Workshop on Linguistic Complexity and Natural Language Processing, pages 59–67
Santa Fe, New Mexico, USA, August 25, 2018.

Besides, usually, two different types of complexity are distinguished: absolute complexity and relative complexity. The absolute complexity is defined as a theoretically-oriented approach which evaluates the complexity of a language-system in a whole sense. On the other hand, the relative complexity takes into account the users of the language to identify the difficulty of processing, learning or acquisition. Other authors such as Blache (Blache, 2011) and Lindstrom (Lindstrom, 2008) distinguish between Global complexity, Local complexity, and Difficulty. *Global complexity* is the absolute perspective of complexity. It aims to provide a number to rank a language as a whole system by means of a degree of complexity. This level is purely theoretical and it does not depend on any kind of linguistic realization. Blache (Blache, 2011) claims that "in Chomskyan terms, this level concern competence", while the local complexity and difficulty belongs to the performance. In contrast, the degree of *local complexity* and *difficulty* are correlated to relative complexity, which is always provided once an input is given. However, local complexity is connected to the linguistic structure and its rules, whereas difficulty is an aspect to take into account for both psycholinguistic approaches and cognitive aspects, which have a role in the complexity evaluation. Within this classification, some authors place grammaticality in difficulty since it is considered a phenomenon of a cognitive aspect from the performance stage. The fact that grammaticality has an important role in the linguistic performance as well as in psycholinguistic approaches is not denied. Nevertheless, in this work, grammaticality is placed as an aspect of the local complexity for two reasons:

- 1) Local complexity is structure-sentence based, and difficulty is speaker-based. In this approach, grammaticality has a tight relation with the structures and the rules of a given input. Consequently, grammaticality belongs to local complexity. However, it has an impact on the difficulty since: the more complex a structure is in terms of grammaticality, the more difficult to process will be.

- 2) The theoretical bases of the Fuzzy Grammar allow us to explain grammaticality by means of the grammar of a language itself, independently of the judgment of the speaker. In this instance, grammaticality is strictly based on the rules of the local complexity.

2.1 Grammaticality as an element of Complexity

Linguistics has been highly influenced by the theoretical fragmentation of Competence - Performance from Chomsky's *Aspects* (Chomsky, 1965). In general, grammaticality has been considered in two ways:

- *A categorical item*: since the competence is perfect, grammaticality can only be either satisfied or violated by means of the speaker or the receiver during the performance stage.

- *A matter of degrees*: grammaticality would be found as a part of an acceptability judgment. This regard considers that grammaticality is not equal to the whole value of an acceptability judgment, and yet it is an essential part which contributes to the total amount of the degree of acceptability from an input. As well as in the last case, here grammaticality belongs to the performance as well.

However, in the Fuzzy Grammar approach, the degree of grammaticality is something which is directly related to the grammar. Grammaticality here does not necessarily come through the speaker, nor through the performance. Once an input is given, the evaluation of the input is in contrast with the grammar of a language itself. The grammaticality value can be totally isolated from the acceptability judgment from either speaker or a receiver. Thus, in this regard, grammaticality is no longer only a psycholinguistic effect. It is also a direct consequence of a structure in relation to its grammar. In this sense, grammaticality would play a role in the degree of relative complexity and local complexity. The Fuzzy Grammar might take into account the complexity of a linguistic structure and its features, such as: number of categories, number of words, number of rules in a structure and degree of grammaticality. In the following section, the base of our fuzzy grammar is going to be defined as well as described in a wider sense.

3 An approach to a Fuzzy Grammar with Fuzzy Descriptions for Complexity

In this section, we will introduce the basics of the formalism used below.

3.1 Introduction to Fuzzy Type Theory

The fuzzy type theory (FTT) was introduced by Novák in (Novák, 2005) which is a higher-order fuzzy logic. Novák further introduced the program of Fuzzy Natural Logic (FNL) (Novák, 2015) as the program for the development of mathematical model of human reasoning that is based on the use of natural language. Its formal background is FTT. Because for applications in linguistics, the most convenient is FTT with a Łukasiewicz algebra of truth values, we will in the sequel refer to it as Ł-FTT.

Let us summarize the basic concepts of FTT and FNL. For more details we refer the reader to the above cited literature.

(a) The algebra of truth values is the standard Łukasiewicz MV_Δ-algebra

$$\mathcal{L} = \langle [0, 1], \vee, \wedge, \otimes, \rightarrow, 0, 1, \Delta \rangle \tag{1}$$

where

$$\wedge = \text{minimum}, \qquad \vee = \text{maximum},$$
$$a \otimes b = \max(0, a + b - 1), \qquad a \rightarrow b = \min(1, 1 - a + b),$$
$$\neg a = a \rightarrow 0 = 1 - a, \qquad \Delta(a) = \begin{cases} 1 & \text{if } a = 1, \\ 0 & \text{otherwise.} \end{cases}$$

(b) The basic concept in FTT is that of a *type*. This is a special subscript (denoted by Greek letters) assigned to all formulas using which we distinguish kinds of objects represented by formulas. The atomic types are ϵ representing elements and o representing truth values. In the semantics is the type ϵ assigned a set M_ϵ whose elements can be anything: people, objects, languages, etc.

(c) The type o (omicron) is the type of truth degree. In the semantics, it is assigned a set of truth values M_o which, in our case, is $M_o = [0, 1]$.[*] The degree of truth $a \in [0, 1]$ may represent various degrees, for example the degree of grammaticality, complexity, etc.

(d) From basic types we form complex ones $\beta\alpha$ where α, β are already formed types. For example, $o\epsilon$, $\epsilon\epsilon$, $(o\epsilon)\epsilon$, $o\alpha$, etc. In the semantics, the complex types $\beta\alpha$ represent *functions*. Thus, each type $\beta\alpha$ is in the semantics assigned as set $M_{\beta\alpha}$ which is a set of functions $M_\alpha \longrightarrow M_\beta$.

(e) Formulas are formed of variables, constants (each of specific type), and the symbol λ. They are denoted by capital letters and assigned a type, i.e., A_α is a formula of type α. In the semantics, A_α is interpreted by some element from the set M_α.

(f) The formula $\equiv$ is the basic connective of *fuzzy equality*. In the semantics, for example, the formula $A_\alpha \equiv B_\alpha$ represents a truth degree of the (fuzzy) equality between the element interpreting A_α and the element interpreting B_α. More concretely, let $\mathcal{M}$ be a semantic interpretation of formulas. Then $\mathcal{M}(A_\alpha) \in M_\alpha$ is an element from the set M_α and similarly, $\mathcal{M}(B_\alpha) \in M_\alpha$ is another element from the same set M_α. Then interpretation $\mathcal{M}(A_\alpha \equiv B_\alpha) \in [0, 1]$ is a truth value of the equality $A_\alpha \equiv B_\alpha$ in the interpretation $\mathcal{M}$.

(g) Semantics of Ł-FTT is defined in a model (or frame), which is the system $\mathcal{M} = <(M_\alpha, \equiv_\alpha)_{\alpha \epsilon Types}>$ where M_α is the set of elements of type $_\alpha$ and $\equiv_\alpha$ is a fuzzy equality on the corresponding set M_α. In other words, explanation of the model consist of couples of sets (fuzzy sets) for all equality. For all infinite sets (M_α) and fuzzy equality $(\equiv)$ exists a type which are connected by the standard Łukasiewicz MV_Δ-algebra. With respect to (a) - (f), $M_o=[0,1]$, M_ϵ is a set due to $\mathcal{M}$, $M_{\beta\alpha}$ is a set of functions due (d) and $\equiv_\alpha$ is interpretation of connective $\equiv$ due to f. Fuzzy equality $\equiv$ on a set M is a fuzzy relation $\equiv$: M x M $\rightarrow$ [0,1].

---

[*] Note that the use of [ ] means any real number/degree between 0 and 1. That could be, e.g., 0.85512 and so on. Note that in classical logic we consider only two truth values, i.e., the set of truth values is $\{0, 1\}$ which means that we consider either 0 (false) or 1 (true).

61

(h) A *fuzzy set* is a function $B : M \longrightarrow [0,1]$ where M is a set having the role of a universe. The function B is often called a *membership function*, i.e., a fuzzy set is identified with its membership function. From the point of view of Ł-FTT, a fuzzy set is obtained as an interpretation of a formula $A_{o\alpha}$ of type α. The universe of such a fuzzy set is then the set M_{α}.

(i) There are several logical connectives in Ł-FTT, namely $\vee$ (disjunction) that is interpreted in the Łukasiewicz algebra by the operation $\vee$ (maximum), $\wedge$ (conjunction) interpreted by $\wedge$ (minimum), & (strong conjunction) interpreted by the operation $\otimes$, $\Rightarrow$ (implication) interpreted by the operation $\rightarrow$ and the special unary connective Δ interpreted by the operation Δ. We introduce also $\neg$ (negation) interpreted by the operation $1 - a$ (cf. item (a)). Besides the logical connectives, also the quantifiers $\forall$ (general quantifier) interpreted by the operation of *infimum* and $\exists$ (existential quantifier) interpreted by the operation of *supremum* are introduced.

(j) The formula $\lambda x_{\alpha} \cdot B_{\beta}$ has the type $\beta\alpha$ and it is interpreted by a function $M_{\alpha} \longrightarrow M_{\beta}$. It says that "each element x_{α} of type α is assigned an element of type β after we substitute the former in the (interpretation of) the formula B_{β}".

(k) The fuzzy type theory has 17 logical axioms and 2 inference rules.

Fuzzy natural logic (FNL) is a mathematical theory that provides models of terms and rules that come with natural language and allow us to reason and argue in it. At the same time, the theory copes with the vagueness of natural language semantics. So far, it is a set of the following formal theories of Ł-FTT:

- A formal theory of evaluative linguistic expressions (Novák, 2008a); see also (Novák, 2007).

- A formal theory of fuzzy IF-THEN rules and approximate reasoning (derivation of a conclusion) (Novák and Lehmke, 2006).

- Formal theory of intermediate and generalized quantifiers (Murinová and Novák, 2016; Novák, 2008b).

3.2 A Fuzzy Grammar structure to explain Degrees of Grammaticality & Complexity

A fuzzy grammar (FGr) is considered as a fuzzy set ($\underset{\sim}{\subseteq}$) on the whole set of rules. These rules define the linguistic knowledge of the fuzzy grammar in every module. We show a fuzzy grammar in a multi-modal sense:

$$FGr \underset{\sim}{\subseteq} Ph_{\alpha} \times Mr_{\beta} \times X_{\gamma} \times S_{\delta} \times L_{\epsilon} \times Pr_{\zeta} \times Ps_{\kappa}$$

A Fuzzy Grammar (FGr) is a fuzzy set which on the Cartesian product of the set of the phonological rules $Ph_{\alpha} = \{ph_{\alpha} \mid ph_{\alpha}$ is a phonological rule$\}$, plus the set of the morphological rules $Mr_{\beta} = \{mr_{\beta} \mid mr_{\beta}$ is a morphological rule$\}$, plus the set of syntactic rules $X_{\gamma} = \{x_{\gamma} \mid x_{\gamma}$ is a syntactic rule), plus the set of semantic rules $S_{\delta} = \{s_{\delta} \mid s_{\alpha}$ is a semantic rule$\}$, plus the set of lexical rules $L_{\epsilon} = \{l_{\epsilon} \mid l_{\epsilon}$ is a lexical rule$\}$, plus the set of pragmatic rules $Pr_{\zeta} = \{pr_{\zeta} \mid pr_{\zeta}$ is a pragmatic rule$\}$, plus the set of prosodic rules $Ps_{\kappa} = \{ps_{\kappa} \mid ps_{\kappa}$ is a prosodic rule$\}$.

We might calculate the absolute complexity of a fuzzy grammar by aggregating membership degrees of the all rules of the grammar. However, we are interested in measuring the complexity of a linguistic structure. We will contrast the rules that define the knowledge of a grammar with another set of rules of an *input* called dialect.

In this regard every dialect would be considered as a language. The dialect is considered here also as a set of rules of an *input* (d_{η}), that is all the rules that are in a dialect's or language's *output*. The set of rules in a dialect can be defined as $D_{\eta} = \{d_{\eta} \mid d_{\eta}$ is a dialect rule$\}$.

Below we provide formalization of a Fuzzy Grammar taking into account an *input* in terms of degrees.

$$FGr \equiv \lambda d_{\eta} \lambda ph_{\alpha} \lambda m_{\beta} \lambda x_{\gamma} \lambda s_{\delta} \lambda l_{\epsilon} \lambda pr_{\zeta} \lambda ps_{\kappa} \cdot (Ph_{(o\eta)\alpha} ph_{\alpha}) d_{\eta} \wedge (Mr_{(o\eta)\beta} mr_{\beta}) d_{\eta} \wedge$$

$$(X_{(o\eta)\gamma}x_\gamma)d_\eta \wedge (S_{(o\delta)\eta}d_\eta)s_\delta \wedge (L_{(o\epsilon)\eta}d_\eta)l_\epsilon \wedge (Pr_{(o\zeta)\eta}d_\eta)pr_\zeta \wedge (Ps_{(o\kappa)\eta}d_\eta)ps_\kappa$$

The syntactic module is taken as an example to explain how this formula works $(X_{(o\eta)\gamma}x_\gamma)d_\eta$. This formula is based in the following reasoning, a function such as $X : X_\gamma \times D_\eta \to M_o$. X (a syntax of a grammar) relates the a set of syntactic rules of a grammar (X_γ) with each rule from the input's dialect (D_η). Therefore, every rule of the syntactic set of rules of an input will match a rule in a dialect. Every matched rule will be linked to a degree in [0,1]. The representation of this is $X_\gamma \to (D_\eta \to M_o)$.

In case a rule is found violated by the dialect, the grammar could trigger another rule to be matched in the dialect. The new triggered rule will match the rule found violated by the dialect and both will be matched with a new degree of grammaticality. An example is provided below.

$Rule_1$, $Rule_2$, $Rule_3$, $Rule_4 \in X_\gamma$ is an example of rules that define the syntax of our fuzzy grammar. $Rule_a$, $Rule_b$, $Rule_c$, $Rule_d \in D_\eta$ is an example of rules that define an input in a dialect.

$$X(Rule_1, Rule_a) = 0.5$$

$$X(Rule_2, Rule_b) = 0.8$$

$$X(Rule_3, Rule_c) = 0.6$$

$$X(Rule_4, Rule_c) = 0.9$$

Every rule from one set is matched to the other one. Consequently, the degree belongs to M_o and it characterizes the relation between the rules of both sets. In this sense, we find degrees of grammaticality in both sets according to one fuzzy grammar.

X ($Rule_3$, $Rule_c$) = 0.6 and X ($Rule_4$, $Rule_c$) = 0.9 is an example of how a rule in a dialect's input trigger two rules in the set of rules of the syntax of a FGr. One is the gold standard rule ($Rule_3$) that has been violated in the dialect ($Rule_c$) and $Rule_4$ is the variability rule which assigns another degree in case the new rule is satisfied in the dialect's *input*.

The operations would be done using the minimum $\wedge$ (Example of minimum a, b 0.5$\wedge$0.4=0.4). This would work in the following way.

$$FGr = \{{}^a/_-< Ph_\alpha, Mr_\beta, X_\gamma, S_\delta, L_\epsilon, Pr_\zeta, Ps_\kappa >, {}^b/_{<...>}, {}^c/_{<...>}\}$$

Here ^{a}, ^{b}, ^{c} are membership degrees (degrees of truth) of the corresponding elements in the angle brackets. The elements in the angle brackets are the modules of the grammar that matched with the elements of the dialect's input as well to a set of degrees.

For example if we extract the degrees from ^{a} and we operate with minimum $\wedge$ it would have the following result: a = 1$\wedge$0.2$\wedge$0.8565$\wedge$0.72$\wedge$0.77$\wedge$1$\wedge$0.97=0.2

In this sense, the degree of grammaticality of both the FGr and a linguistic module will be always depend on the relation between the identified rules and its degrees. The grammatical knowledge (competence) of a set takes into account the variables in a grammar in terms of degrees (if an input is satisfied or violated and its degree) but, obviously, the degree of grammaticality of an input only can be triggered by a dialect's input in relation to a grammar. Therefore, the degree of grammaticality is always related to the set of rules of a fuzzy grammar (knowledge of a language).

The local complexity will be measured in terms of degrees by the linguistic knowledge represented by the membership degree in the FGr. This distance will be related to how close is the *input* of a dialect to the fuzzy grammar in terms of grammaticality.

Consequently, the more constraints that are satisfied in a grammar by a given input, the more grammatical it will be. Therefore, a given input has a high value of grammaticality according to its grammar (and not by the speaker's perception). A given input which respects the structures and the rules of a grammar will have a high grammaticality value. A given input which triggers a lot of violations will display more complex rules and structures for a grammar since those structures either require more specific rules or simply those rules do not belong to the grammar which is evaluating the input. Therefore, the higher the value of grammaticality in an input, the lower the value of its complexity.

4 Property Grammars: A contraint-based theory for dealing with Fuzziness & Gradience

Regarding fuzzy grammar, Blache's (Blache, 2000), (Blache, 2005), (Blache, 2016) Property Grammars have been chosen as the formal theoretical framework in defining natural language fuzziness and variability. This theory combines a full-constraint framework of independent and flexible constraints (or properties), with syntactic dependencies under the notion of construction from Construction Grammars. Constructions have been described in terms of their properties. Property Grammars display several constraints in order to describe the syntactic relations between local language phenomena. However, here we focus on the following ones:

- *Linearity* ($>$): Precedence order between two elements. A precedes B.

- *Requirement* ($\leftrightarrow$): Co-occurrence between two elements: A requires B.

- *Exclusion* (excl.): A and B never appear in co-occurrence in the specified construction.

5 An example of Relative Complexity within the boundaries of a Fuzzy Grammar

<table>
<tr><td colspan="2">Pronoun in Subject Construction</td></tr>
<tr><td>1</td><td>CnW1: [Neutral Demonstratives; Relatives Pronouns; Personal Pronouns]</td></tr>
<tr><td colspan="2">SYNTAX CANONICAL PROPERTIES</td></tr>
<tr><td colspan="2">PRON excl. PREP∧ADJ∧ADV∧DET∧PRON</td></tr>
<tr><td colspan="2">SYNTAX VARIABLE PROPERTIES</td></tr>
<tr><td>V1: PRON excl. ADJ</td><td>PRON SxPt 2
PRON↔ADJ: [solo] or [mismo]</td></tr>
<tr><td>V2: PRON excl. Det</td><td>PRON↔[yo]
D↔[el]
PRON↔fit NOUN SxPt</td></tr>
<tr><td>2</td><td>CnW 0.5: [lo]</td></tr>
<tr><td colspan="2">SYNTAX CANONICAL PROPERTIES</td></tr>
<tr><td colspan="2">PRON>ADJ
PRON↔ADJ
PRON excl. PREP ∧ DET ∧ ADV</td></tr>
<tr><td colspan="2">VabW 0.5 [Non PRON in PRON fit]</td></tr>
<tr><td colspan="2">SYNTAX VARIABLE PROPERTIES</td></tr>
<tr><td>1</td><td>NPPF↔PREP [mod]
NPPF > [de]</td></tr>
<tr><td>2</td><td>NPPF↔ADJ</td></tr>
</table>

Figure 1: Pronoun's Syntactic Properties in Subject Construction.

The symbols and concepts presented in Figure 1 are explained here[†]:

a *Syntactic Canonical Properties*: These are the properties which define the gold standard of the Fuzzy Grammar.

b *Syntactic Variability Properties*: These properties are triggered in the fuzzy grammar only when a violation is identified in an input. They explain syntactic variability.

[†]From now, Greek symbols are not related with previous sections

(c) *Cnw*: It refers to the *Canonical Weight* of a rule in a Grammar. It is understood as the gold standard. We will use α to identify it.

(d) *V*: It means *Violation* and it points out the property that has been violated. Pointing out the violation of a property is necessary in order to trigger the related syntactic variability properties. The violability weight will be identified as β.

(e) *VabW*: It means the *Variability Weight*. This weight balances the grammaticality value by adding another value and, therefore, softening the violation. The Variability Weight will be identified as γ.

(f) $\wedge$ has no value as operator and it is understood as "and".

(g) The brackets [ ] are used to mark the elements which are defined in terms of properties.

(h) *NPPF* refers to a linguistic element which is not a pronoun but it has a pronoun fit.

Figure 1 is a sample of a gradient description of fuzziness and variability in a Fuzzy Grammar with properties. We show the formal description of the PRON [pronoun]. Neutral Demonstrative, Relatives and Personal Pronouns are the canonical ones regarding our corpus (Universal Dependency Spanish Treebank Corpus 2.0). The most canonical structure is weighted as 1, a medium canonical is weighted as 0.5, a violation is weighted as -1 and recurrent variability has a 0.5 weight[‡]. The framework can describe inputs with grammatical violations and their syntactic variability. The fuzzy phenomenon is explained with a double analysis:

(1) First Phase: *Syntactic Canonical Properties*

(2) Second Phase: *Syntactic Variability Properties*

Firstly, a normal parsing is applied. This parser describes the syntactic properties considering only the canonical ones (the gold standard). The result of this parsing describes both satisfied and violated canonical properties. The canonical deviations with its violations will be defined in terms of properties. The value of the addition between α and β will be divided by the Total amount of Part of Speech (δ). A value of complexity in terms of grammaticality is provided here (VG_1: Value of Grammaticality 1):

$$VG_1 = \frac{\alpha + \beta}{\delta} \tag{2}$$

Secondly, the parser runs for a second time, taking into account the violations and defining the Syntactic Variability Properties. In case some Syntax Property is violated, such as V1 or V2, Syntactic Variability Properties are triggered. Their weight of violability is going to be mitigated in case the violation respects these new properties. If the new properties are not satisfied, variability is not going to have any effect here and β would remain as before. After this second analysis, a new value will be provided (VG_2: Value of Grammaticality 2) following the formula in (3).

$$VG_2 = \frac{(\beta + \gamma) + \alpha}{\delta} \tag{3}$$

This system also works for explaining words which undergo a partial transition in terms of part of speech. These transitions concern fuzzy boundaries in parts of speech. The more transitions the more complex an input will be. Thus, we would assume that the word-class does not undergo a complete transition of membership, but more of context. This explains why other properties must be taken into account regarding variability.

Several D [determiner] (especially articles and demonstratives) occur as PRON quite often, but never as often as they occur as a D (articles: 73.10%; demonstratives: 10,44% in more than 4000 occurrences).

[‡]Note that these weights illustrate a basic idea of gradience. They are not related to the real weights of gradience in Spanish syntax. A precise value of gradience for each weight in each set or construction will be established in the future. We emphasize that this is currently in progress.

If those D ever appear as a PRON this framework detects a violation in the first parsing since, canonically, a D must precede N [Noun]. In the second parsing, the following Syntactic Variability Properties in the determiner will be triggered clarifying how it is possible to have a determiner without a NOUN:

$$Syntactic\,Variability\,Properties : Determiner\ \neg(D > N)\ \Longleftrightarrow\ PRON\gamma_{1\vee 2}$$

In words: Syntactic Variability Properties are triggered once a Determiner violates ($\neg$) the property $D > N$, therefore the input have to satisfy the properties found in the Syntactic Variability Properties of the PRON (PRONγ) either the first one (1) or the second one (2). The symbol $\Longleftrightarrow$ is used since the syntactic variability properties are true only when both elements co-occur at the same time.

Because the new fit in this case is a PRON, we describe their properties in the PRON. The same happens in V2 where PRON undergo a fit transition to the NOUN syntactic properties and thus, their new properties are located in Noun Construction. In V1 occurs something similar but in a softer way, in which PRON undergo a transition to the properties of the canonical PRON case number 2 [lo].

6 Final remarks

Local Complexity is dependent on an input's rules and structure. The Fuzzy Grammar takes into account what happens when a sentence has rules which are satisfied or violated. A given input has a value of grammaticality according to its grammar (and not by the speaker's perception). The more constraints that are satisfied, the more grammatical it will be. An input which triggers a lot of violations is going to display more variable rules in the fuzzy grammar (as it was shown in the example of the pronoun). The process of a double parsing for variability rules would increase the complexity of the given sentences. In this sense, the lower the value of grammaticality, the higher the value of complexity for a determinate grammar. Besides, the input with violations would probably be more ambiguous, as shown in the example of the pronoun. Therefore, yet more complex.

Some theories in complexity establish that the more rules there are in a sentence, the more complex a sentence is. Actually, in this proposed approach, the complexity of a sentence might be mitigated or reduced in case the grammar rules are satisfied.

7 Acknowledgement

This research has been supported by the Ministerio de Economía y Competitividad and the Fondo Europeo de Desarrollo Regional under the project number FFI2015-69978-P (MINECO/FEDER, UE) of the Programa Estatal de Fomento de la Investigación Científica y Técnica de Excelencia, Subprograma Estatal de Generación de Conocimiento.

References

Bas Aarts. 2004. Conceptions of gradience in the history of linguistics. *Language Sciences*, 26(4):343–389.

Philippe Blache. 2000. Property Grammars and the Problem of Constraint Satisfaction. *Proc. of ESSLLI 2000 workshop on Linguistic Theory and Grammar Implementation*, pages 47–56.

Philippe Blache. 2005. Property Grammars: A Fully Constraint-based Theory. *Constraint Solving and Language Processing*, 3438:1–16.

Philippe Blache. 2011. A computational model for linguistic complexity. *Biology, Computation and Linguistics.*, 288:155–167.

Philippe Blache. 2016. Representing Syntax by Means of Properties : a Formal Framework for Descriptive Approaches. *Journal of Language Modelling*, 4(2):183–224.

Dwight Le Merton Bolinger. 1961. *Generality: Gradience and the All-or-none*. Mouton & Company, 14 edition.

Noam Chomsky. 1965. *Aspects of the theory of syntax*. Cambridge: MIT Press.

Östen Dahl. 2004. *The growth and maintenance of linguistic complexity*, volume 71. John Benjamins Publishing.

Frank Keller. 2000. *Gradience in grammar: Experimental and computational aspects of degrees of grammaticality*. Ph.D. thesis, Edinburgh: University of Edinburgh.

Eva Lindstrom. 2008. Language complexity and interlinguistic difficulty. *Language Complexity: Typology, Contact, Change*, 94:217.

John H. Mc Worther. 2001. The world's simpliest grammars are creole grammars. *Linguistic Typology*, (5).

Petra Murinová and Vilm Novák. 2016. Syllogisms and 5-square of opposition with intermediate quantifiers in fuzzy natural logic. *Logica universalis*, 10(2):339–357.

Vilm Novák and Stephan Lehmke. 2006. Logical structure of fuzzy IF-THEN rules. *Fuzzy Sets and Systems*, 157:2003–2029.

Vilm Novák. 2005. On fuzzy type theory. *Fuzzy Sets and Systems*, 149:235–273.

Vilm Novák. 2007. Mathematical fuzzy logic in modeling of natural language semantics. In P. Wang, D. Ruan, and E.E. Kerre, editors, *Fuzzy Logic – A Spectrum of Theoretical & Practical Issues*, pages 145–182. Elsevier, Berlin.

Vilm Novák. 2008a. A comprehensive theory of trichotomous evaluative linguistic expressions. *Fuzzy Sets and Systems*, 159(22):2939–2969.

Vilm Novák. 2008b. A formal theory of intermediate quantifiers. *Fuzzy Sets and Systems*, 159(10):1229–1246.

Vilém Novák. 2015. Fuzzy natural logic: Towards mathematical logic of human reasoning. In *Towards the Future of Fuzzy Logic*, pages 137–165. Springer.

Lotfi A. Zadeh. 1965. Fuzzy sets. *Information and control*, 8(3):338–353.

Lofti A. Zadeh. 1972. A fuzzy-set-theoretic interpretation of linguistic hedges. *Journal of Cybernetics*, 2(3):4–34.

Author Index